THE LAND, THE LANGUAGE, AND THE LORE

COMPRISE

THE FIFTH GOSPEL

NELSON L. PRICE

A Primer Travel Guide to the Holy Land

Dr. Nelson L. Price

All Rights Reserved

ISBN-13: 978-0-9671696-7-5
ISBN-10: 0-9671696-7-4

Price: $14.95

First Edition
Manufactured in the USA

Copyright @ 2018

**Inquiries regarding bulk purchases or
discounts should be addressed to:**

Dr. Nelson L. Price
1400 Beaumont Drive
Kennesaw, Georgia 30152
Phone: (770) 422-2564
Fax: (770) 427-6578

**E-Mail: NLPrice31@att.com
www.nelsonprice.com**

To understand the Bible better

is to better understand the Bible.

ACKNOWLEDGEMENTS

An author is the nexus of individuals and elements who inspire and enable a book. These factors are numerous regarding this work. To each, the author is deeply indebted and most grateful. I offer tribute and thanks to all who have been so helpful:

My wife, Trudy, my loving companion on forty-four trips to the Bible Land, and the first editor of this work.

Clay Corvin, whose encouragement and support motivated and enabled this writing.

Terry and Nelda Moore, whose crafting and proofing greatly enriched this work.

To these and many others who made direct and indirect contributions, I thank you.

Nelson L. Price

CONTENTS

THE LANGUAGE AND THE LORE

PREFACE

This book is written in response to the many questions which members of tourist groups to the Bible Land have posed through the years. Each topic included within *The Fifth Gospel* merits a volume of exhaustive information; however, this work is an attempt to give a succinct overview of issues. In that sense, it is a *"Light,"* concise primer: *Light* because God has empowered its writing, *concise* out of its practical intent, and *primer* because it is written primarily in lay language for the everyday visitor to the Land of the Bible, not written with a primary intent of sharing new scholarship.

This book is offered with the prayer it will aid persons in the understanding of the Bible.

It has as its target audience three groups:

- Those who are going to visit the Bible Land and desire insight into what to expect.
- Those who have visited the Bible Land and want a better understanding of what they saw and heard.
- Those who will never visit the Bible Land, but would like a virtual trip to the Bible Land in order to better understand the Bible.

Every thought has a background. A knowledge of the setting, the spokesman, and the sphere from which a thought emerges helps to bring understanding to the concept. Its milieu, both in the mundane and the profound, gives experiences and words meaning. In photography, the background helps define and make clear the foreground, giving greater clarity and depth to a picture. And words necessarily are impacted by background for their meaning and specificity. For instance, in an aquatic setting, a *dive* refers to a method of entering a pool of water. In a culinary setting, *dive* defines a type of eating establishment. And, in America, *boot* and *bonnet* refer to footwear and headwear. In South Africa, bonnet refers to the hood of a car and boot, the trunk. In all communication, background, meaning, and message are inextricably linked.

Just as the background and people serve to define a singular word, so does an understanding of the lore and history of a locale impact interpretation of words and events. In the theological realm also—and *especially* in Scriptural matters, knowing the background of the Bible Land, the meaning of specific language, and the lore that has grown up around historical events can bring greater clarity to and comprehension of the events and people of the Bible. The time, place, and traditions in which the Bible was authored give immense and indispensable present-day insight into its meaning. And because meanings of words and perceptions of events sometime change from one generation to another, knowing the original intent can more accurately guide present-day perception. That is the goal of this book: to introduce to the first-time visitor—or to confirm for the reader—the profound relationship between the biblical land and the message which the Holy Book has held for humanity throughout the generations.

May a better understanding of the

LAND, LANGUAGE, AND LORE

aid the reader's conception and

comprehension of the Bible.

THE LAND OF HALLOWED LIGHT

On the first day of creation, God said, Let there be light. ~**Genesis 1: 3**

Something there is to ponder about the Light that has enveloped and hovered over God's creation since the Beginning. While the abstract, impersonal concept of God, the Light, enveloping His earth and His people is comforting, there is even greater comfort, even exhilaration, in current research which confirms that, again, Believers can find literal, tangible, and eternal Truth in the very words of the Bible.

It is true that Truth is proclaimed through many formats in the Bible: analogies, proverbs, narratives, poetry, prophecy. These many forms of literature are often perceived as abstractions to teach concrete Christian outcomes. And largely, the words—perhaps with the exception of the many prophecies which have been validated—have existed somewhat muted by the presumption of abstraction requiring interpretation before application.

Certainly, that application-via-interpretation approach to Bible learning has provided a strong Christian community through the generations. But while the muted, veiled approach to reading the words of the Bible has rendered positive outcomes, perhaps Christians simultaneously have overlooked Truth which is actually trumpeted about the Presence of God in His creation—His people, His Earth...His Holy Land. The reality of God's Presence—of God's Light—in the entire cosmos is now declared to be literal, declared through current scientific research.

Laboratory experiments have recently made tangible the proclamation of God as Light in Genesis 1:3. While the terminology and methods of the recent scientific investigation of light are tedious and best understood by those with advanced scientific training, the conclusion of the study is profound and clear for an empirical validation of the long-presumed spiritual abstraction of God.

Light as a tangible, personal Luminary entity now has become a scientific reality—an astounding validation of the Truth of the Bible, a physical validation of God. The key is found in the Hebrew word *owr* in *Genesis 1:3,* meaning luminescent energy or electromagnetic waves (EM), which are caused by the oscillation of electric and magnetic fields. The frequency of the electromagnetic waves determines the form of waves.

The sections of the (EM) spectrum ranging from the lower to the greater are gamma rays, X-rays, ultraviolet radiation, visible light, infrared radiation, and radio waves. Though all are not discernible to the human eye, these are all forms of light. The human eye can only see light with a band of 430-770 terahertz (THz) frequency called the visible spectrum.

The sidebar question explored in recent experiments was this: Can light be transformed into matter? The answer has experimentally been proven to be yes. Visible light as well as all other forms of electromagnetic radiation like X-rays, radio waves, and microwaves are carried by photons. *All* electromagnetic waves are the reference in Genesis 1: 3. Both visible and invisible forms are, in reality, light. In an experiment as early as 1934, two American physicists, Gregory Breit and John A. Wheeler, theorized that if one could make two protons collide, the collision would produce two positron-electron pairs—and thus convert light into matter.

Science has now progressed to the point where two experiments, one by the Imperial College of London and one by Stanford's linear collider, have proven that light can be converted into matter. It is significant that God created the light first, saying, "Let there be light" (Genesis 1:3). Then he created the lesser lights of the sun and the moon and the firmament (Genesis 1: 14-16). It is evident that light itself was created first, before the lesser lights, obviously establishing a separation, a difference, in the creation of the light and the lights. Dr. George F. Smoot III, Nobel Prize winning physicist, validated the first light of creation. He conducted an experiment for the Cosmic Background Explorer (COBE) that resulted in the measurement "of the black body form and anisotropy of the cosmic microwave background radiation." He spoke of the finding as showing the first light of creation. Of it he said, "It was like looking at the face of God."

As true science continues to unfold, objective and verifiable data will surely continue to validate the truth of God's Presence in His Creation—and even the proof of God Himself as Light. What science might conclude ultimately is that the light Smoot made tangible *is* "looking at the face of God," not "*like* looking at the face of God." And based upon the eternal Truth of the Bible, the light that the researcher "touched" was not merely the radiance *of* God or the radiance *from* God. The radiance *was* God. God, by His own declaration, *is* the Luminary from Whom comes the luminescence. For it was Jesus Himself—God Incarnate—Who said, "I am the light of the world."

I am the Light....

Throughout the generations, most theologians have taken Jesus' words in the abstract and have commendably constructed a powerful, irrefutable theology even from the presumed abstractions, but how exhilarating, how spine-tingling that God's Word is also very literal. As is certain to become progressively clearer through true science, much of what Scripture says is literal—yes, literal as in prophetic events, but also literal for this very moment of time.

In the light of long-acknowledged biblical truth—and now in view of current-day scientific validation, Christian pilgrims can visit the Bible Land with a new enthusiasm, a new certainty. God's Light is and always has been that tangible, literal Light, the luminescence emanating from the face of God that today infuses His creation—and the *promised* land, its *chosen* people, and its events throughout all times. It was in this land where Jesus, God's Son—God *Himself*— entered History to redeem humanity from sin and death. Here, the luminescence *from* God permeates the sites and the history of the land—the Holy Land. It is the power and presence of this Living Light which compel throngs of people to visit the land to learn more of the Bible and perhaps to worship in baptism in the Jordan in imitation of

Jesus Himself. The power and presence of the Light hallow the land where Jesus walked and where He taught and where he died for the redemption of His earth.   And... hallow the land, even to the specificity of the Mount of Olives, where Jesus the Light of the World will return to conclude His redemption of fallen humanity.

He who is the blessed and only Sovereign, the King of kings and Lord of lords, who alone had immortality, dwelling in unapproachable light, whom no man has seen or can see, to whom be honor and everlasting power. Amen.

~ I Timothy 6: 15, 16

THE ACQUISITION OF THE LAND

"...a land for which the Lord your God cares; the eyes of the Lord your God are always on it, from the beginning of the year to the very end of the year." ~ **Deuteronomy 11: 12**

The land of modern Israel formed the stage on which the God Drama played out. Here, Immanuel began His earth walk. Before the Advent, the stage had to be set. No region of earth has been inhabited by more varied ethnic groups. Jebusites, Canaanites, Philistines from Crete, Amorites, Edomites, Nabateans, Arameans, Arabs, Greeks, Romans, and European crusaders are a microcosm of the cultures. Among those, perhaps two made the most significant impact of any outside groups.

After conquering the Persian empire of Darius III, Alexander the Great conquered Jerusalem without difficulty on his way to Egypt in 332 BC.

As a lad in Macedonia, Alexander and his father, King Philip of Macedonia, watched a battle played out using a new military tactic called a phalanx. It became the strategy by which he conquered his homeland. In seeking to organize a larger army with men from various regions, he realized there was a language barrier. Therefore, he called his scholars together and ordered them to construct a new Greek language more perfect and exact. He spread this Attic-Ionic language everywhere he went. It became the standard language in commerce and government. Because Alexander spoke Attic, it was the language that spread. As it spread, it interacted with other languages and evolved into the more common form of Koine Greek. It was to become the basis of the language in which the accounts of the New Testament would be written. The Greeks who remained in the land made their language popular throughout the region.

Upon invading Israel, Alexander viewed Jerusalem from Mount Scopus. The priests came out with their scrolls which they used to convince him their prophet Daniel had foretold his coming. Thus, they won his favor, and he carried many Jews with him on further conquests. He also left behind in the land numerous Greeks and Greek-speaking people who made their language popular. This became vital in preparation for the writing of the New Testament. A number of the apostles had Greek names: Philip, John, Peter, and Mark, for example, as did Paul. Luke was born a Greek in Antioch, Syria.

A second aspect of the setting of the stage involved a decree which went out from Caesar Augustus on Capitoline Hill in Rome. It ordered all citizens of the regions of Rome to return to the home of their origin and register in order to be taxed. That put into motion all the rivers of prophecy regarding Messiah flowing into the lake of fulfillment in Bethlehem.

From Bethlehem's grotto where "the Word became flesh and came and dwelt among us" to the caves of Nazareth, from Mount Zion to the Valley of the Shadow of Death, from synagogues to the seaside, life's lessons were taught, and "the way, the truth, and the life" became clear.

From the azure blue waters of the Great Sea to the emerald green waters of the Jordan River, from the summit of the Mount of Transfiguration to the depths of the Jordan Valley, from Dan to Beersheba, love rained down.

A mountainside in Galilee became an amphitheater where a voice with a certain intonation, resonance, and clarity spoke as never a man had spoken. Reason grappled with irrationality and won.

Here the lilies of the field, the birds of the air, the fishes of the sea, and a city set on a hill became object lessons.

Here the clarion voice of truth was heard, not to be drowned out by vitriolic shouts. From the barren sands of the Wilderness of Judea to the bustling urban streets, love was domiciled in flesh and blood.

Here God—with an epidermis, a twinkle in His eye, cheer in His voice, and a spring in His step—walked on the waters of the Sea of

Galilee and the limestone cobblestone of old Jerusalem.

Here His red blood stained the gray stones of Calvary before the Judean winds had covered His footprints in the sands.

At a place called Calvary, death's dirge seemed to have drowned out life's song. Sorrow's leash was unloosed. Its sickening influence choked reason blind. The Vine had withered, the Branch had died, the Bread of Life became food for mold, the Rose of Sharon faded, the Lily of the Valley lost its bloom, and the Light of the World was extinguished.

From a sepulcher outside the city walls, Christ arose from the dead. Out of the cold tomb that enveloped His lifeless form came the vindicated Victor, the bodily resurrected living Lord Jesus Christ. That was the day death died as the demons wept and the angels rejoiced.

When it seemed that his lips stilled by death were eternally mute, He arose to proclaim, "I am He who was dead and am alive, and I live forevermore."

Matthew, Mark, Luke, and John became the penmen to write the four gospels revealing this great love epoch. The land resonates with revelations explaining the biblical account. To better understand the four gospels, throngs of people visit the land which, in the fourth century, Jerome was the first to call the FIFTH GOSPEL. There is no better commentary on the four gospels. The topography, traditions, habitudes, ethics, mores, and taboos of the land that form the setting for the Scripture help interpret it. The land, the language, and the lore assure a greater understanding of the Scripture.

As historically there has been imbrication of cultures, so a visitor reading *The Fifth Gospel* today has to be prepared mentally to look beyond current conditions and envision the biblical events and sites in their setting. To get the most out of visiting the land, it is essential to compartmentalize personal thoughts—that is, to mentally and emotionally see through the present surface veneer, live the moment of the historical happening, be spiritually prepared to close out distractions, and focus on using *The Fifth Gospel* as a practical guide.

JESUS' BIRTH

Nestled in the mountains of Galilee was the tiny village of Nazareth. It was so small and insignificant that none of the Jewish sources of the first and second centuries listing the towns and villages of Galilee include it. Little wonder that later in life, Nathaniel asked the question, "Can anything good come out of Nazareth?"

Then, as today in the Bible Land, some people lived in caves. Nazareth was principally populated by fewer than two hundred cave dwellers consisting of twenty to thirty families. The settlement was only a few hundred yards long. They would have had no furniture, and most implements would have been stone or pottery. A catacomb of caves runs under modern Nazareth. At one time they served as a sanctuary for persons hiding from the Romans.

Each family would have had its own cave adapted to its liking. Some would have had two chambers, one above the other with the animals in the lower chamber and the living quarters above. The heat from the animals would have risen through a shaft connecting the two.

Each would have had a small plot of land on which to grow olive trees, a few sheep, and barley. Wheat does not grow well in the rocky soil.

The stone around Nazareth is soft limestone that made enlarging a cave easier. Some caves had a small room built of stone as an entrance.

There is no well in the Bible account of an angel appearing to Mary. However, today a Greek Orthodox Church has been built over the spring of Nazareth. Later apocryphal writings depict Mary being at the well when she was visited by the angel.

Mary became only the second person to whom an angel had appeared in over four hundred years. The message was "The Holy Spirit will come upon you, and the power of the Highest will overshadow you; therefore, also, the Holy One who is to be born will be called the Son of God" (Luke 1: 35).

During the Old Testament era, the Holy Spirit did work in the lives of a very select few, but the doctrine of the Holy Spirit was not taught. Lacking knowledge of the Holy Spirit, the response of Mary and her family is all the more remarkable.

Imagine Mary going home to tell her mother, "Mother, I am pregnant."

"You are what? By whom?"

"By the Holy Spirit."

"The Holy What?"

From the beginning, Mary's explanation would be questioned. This would have been further complicated by word circulating among the gossips of Nazareth.

MARY'S VISIT WITH ELIZABETH

Mary, a godly young woman, knew the laws of her day. She knew that as soon as her presumed adultery was known she would be carried to the priest, condemned, and executed immediately. A modest, virtuous young woman would have tried to hide her pregnancy. However, the first thing Mary did was visit her cousin Elizabeth, who was married to Zacharias, the officiating high priest in the Temple. Mary confided in Elizabeth. Customs of the day would have required Elizabeth to tell her husband. In Israel there were more than twenty thousand priests. There were twenty-five courses of priests, with each course having eight thousand priests. Zacharias was in course number eight. It was their turn to serve. Out of eight thousand priests, one was chosen by drawing lots to serve burning incense in the Holy of Holies (Luke 1: 9). Zacharias was the one chosen.

In the solitude of the Holy of Holies, an angel of the Lord appeared to Zacharias and told him of the forthcoming birth of His own son, John the Baptist, whose role it would be to serve as the forerunner of Messiah, whose birth the angel also foretold. This dramatic revelation convinced him Mary was telling the truth about her conception being of the Holy Spirit. This restrained him from seeking her execution.

BETROTHAL

Mary and Joseph were betrothed at the time. This constituted the parents of a couple entering into a contract for their children to be wed. Joseph would have paid the bride price to her father. A formal contract would have been signed known as a *shiddukin*. Also signed would have been the *tenaim*, which defined the conditions of the contract. At this time, the couple was considered betrothed, which was the same as being wed, but with a principal difference. During the betrothal, though officially wed, they lived apart with their families for a year without cohabitation. Soon thereafter they began their trek to Bethlehem.

Concurrent with the approaching birth, a decree went out from Caesar Augustus that necessitated the journey. All persons were required to go to their ancestral homes to register and be taxed.

Though Mary and Joseph were from Nazareth, their ancestral home was Bethlehem. It is commonly held that when the Assyrians conquered Galilee in 733 BC, they did as was their custom and relocated the entire population to other territories. The land was virtually uninhabited for six hundred years. After this time, people began to gravitate into the territory. Some immigrants were people from Judah, hence Bethlehem. Among them were the ancestors of Mary and Joseph.

The Bible account of the approaching birth of Jesus Christ tells us all we need to know, but not as much as we would like to know. Some extra-biblical sources help fill in the blanks. Reliable records of customs and conditions of the time help the pieces fit together.

Artists, not the Bible, depict Joseph leading a donkey ridden by Mary on their journey to Bethlehem. Not so. Donkeys were for village and urban use, not journeys. Camels were for commerce; horses were for the wealthy and Romans. It is highly likely the poor couple had no animal but walked. If they had had an animal, it would have been a mule. Mules were in common use for such purposes.

Mary and Joseph in their journey would have left Nazareth and rendezvoused with a group at the south end of the Sea of Galilee. Robbers and wild animals made it essential to travel in groups. Small militias were paid to escort groups.

The ninety-mile trip would have taken six or seven days. After leaving the Sea of Galilee, they would have concluded their first day's journey at the pagan city of Beit She'an where they would have camped outside of the city. Beit She'an was a large city in the hills of Gilboa where the Philistines brought the headless bodies of Saul and Jonathan for display on the walls of the city after their final battle.

Here Mary and Joseph would have crossed to the east bank of the Jordan and walked for four days through the area of Perea, governed by Antipas, to Jericho, where they would have crossed back over a bridge to the western bank. At the bridge, they would have encountered the hostility of the people of Judea who detested Galileans. Offensive Roman soldiers were always at the bridge searching travelers and looking for Zealots. Contact with the Romans, who were pagans, would have defiled them, making them ceremonially unclean.

It was in this vicinity where John the Baptist would later baptize Jesus.

From here, they would have had two of the hardest days of their journey. From Jericho to Jerusalem, there were always a number of hostile Roman soldiers.

They would have ascended to Bethlehem through the Wilderness of Judah by way of a deep, foreboding, perilous valley named years before by David as the Valley of the Shadow of Death. That ascent would have been approximately two thousand feet.

QUIRINIUS, GOVERNOR OF SYRIA

The Gospel of Luke records Jesus was born when "Quirinius

was governing Syria" (Luke 2: 2). This is a marker helping to define the time of Jesus' birth. However, it presents challenges. Luke also notes this was the time "a decree went out from Caesar Augustus that all the world should register."

A casual reading of the events gives the impression there is a conflict in the dates.

Herod would have been responsible for implementing the census commanded by Augustus. Such a decree was imposed in 2 BC. Herod died between 4 and 1 BC.

One appointment of Quirinius was made in 6 BC. Thus, these dates conflict. This leads to many assuming there is a conflict in the Scripture.

Luke says the birth occurred during "the first enrollment," which distinguishes it from the more often noted one in 6 BC.

It should be noted the Scripture says Quirinius was "governing Syria," not "was governor of Syria." The term used for governing, *hegemon*, not only referred to the official governor of a state, but to anyone in a lesser office such as legate, prelate, or delegate acting with imperial authority. He simply might have been appointed on a special authoritative mission. The term used by Luke could be applied to any Roman official of lesser authority. Quirinius at different times governed in various roles and actually served twice as the governor.

The historian Josephus notes, "Quirinius, a Roman senator who had gone through other magistracies, and had passed through them all until he had become consul, was appointed governor of Syria by Caesar and was given the task of assessing property there and in Judea."

It was during his career he would have been responsible for enforcing the census and Jesus was born.

LINEAGE

Two genealogies of Jesus are given in Scripture that vary

greatly. Two explanations are offered to reconcile the accounts:

- Luke (3: 23 - 38) starts with Jesus and traces the lineage back through Mary to Adam.
- Matthew (1: 1 - 16) starts with Abraham and traces the lineage down through David and Joseph to Jesus.

Eusebius, a church historian, suggests Matthew is tracing the primary biological lineage and Luke takes in account the levirate marriage laws of the day. Under this code of law, if a man died without having a son, the man's brother was to marry the widow and have a son who would bear the deceased brother's name. Based upon this, Eusebius, postulates Melchi (Luke 3: 24) and Matthan (Matthew 1: 15) were married to the same woman at different times. Thus, Heli (Luke 3: 23) and Jacob (Matthew 1: 15) would be half-brothers. Upon the death of Heli without a son, his brother Jacob would have married the widow of Heli, who gave birth to Joseph. Hence, Joseph, the "son of Heli," was biologically the legal "son of Jacob."

Matthew and Luke both are recording the same genealogy, but Luke follows the legal lineage and Matthew the biological.

There is another possible resolution which suggests Luke is recording Mary's genealogy and Matthew, Joseph's. Matthew follows the line of Joseph, Jesus' legal father, through David's son Solomon. Luke follows the line of Mary, Jesus' biological mother, through David's son Nathan. There being no Greek word for son-in-law, Joseph is referred to as the "son of Heli" by virtue of his marriage to Mary, Heli's daughter. Through the bloodline of Joseph or Mary, Jesus was a descendant of David and prophetically qualified to be Messiah. In that era, it was most unusual to trace a child's lineage through the mother. It is done in this instance to doubly evidence Jesus' role as Messiah.

The lineage of Messiah is specifically given in order to identify Jesus as the Messiah. All birth records in that time that would reveal Jesus to be Messiah were kept in the Temple. When the Temple was destroyed, so were the records. If Messiah was not born prior to that, there is no way his lineage could be traced.

THE TIME OF JESUS' BIRTH

The exact date of the birth of Jesus is difficult to determine. When He was born the western world was using a calendar dated from the founding of the city of Rome AUC, meaning in the year of the founded city. It continued to be used for five hundred years after the birth of Jesus. During the sixth century, an eminent scholarly monk named Dionysius Exiguus proposed a new calendar be adopted based on the birth of Jesus. The Christian world adopted it immediately. General acceptance was much slower. It was not approved in England until the end of the seventh century. Only in the fifteenth century was it adopted universally. In making the transition from AUC to BC, Dionysius made a mistake of several years.

Based on the date of the death of Herod the Great, Jesus was likely born between 7 and 4 BC.

The exact time of His birth is not known. It is said it could not have been in December because shepherds are not in the fields at night watching their sheep. That alone does not negate the possibility of a December birth. A group of American tourists were sitting around an open fire in Shepherd's Field. Illumined by the light of the full moon an old shepherd emerged followed by his sheep. It was 10:15 PM, December 25, 1974, proving shepherds are sometimes in their fields at night in December.

The birth might very well have been in September. Historically, shepherds have taken advantage of plant growth deep in the Judean desert in the winter to let their sheep browse there. This lets the vegetation in the hills regrow, allowing for summer grazing.

The shepherds would have been in the hills near Bethlehem at that time. Sheep mate when daylight wanes in the autumn, and the lambs are born in the spring. During the mating season, shepherds are in the fields watching their flocks to separate those that have mated from the others. After the mating season has passed, the shepherds lead their flocks to lower elevations.

THE STAR

A second condition suggesting the birth might have been in September is the star followed by the Wise Men. At that time in history, astronomy was called astrology without the modern connotation. As astronomers, they gave spiritual significance to the stars and their alignment.

Various explanations have been given regarding such a celestial sentinel. Scripture says God created the stars of which there are two hundred billion in the galaxy. It is said, "He counts the stars, He calls them all by name" (Psalm 148:3).

It is now conceded that those who devised the calendar were off in setting the year with which to begin. That is not a negative reflection on Scripture. Herod was alive when the star appeared, and the commonly quoted date of his death is 4 BC. Thus, the star would have occurred between 7 BC and 4 BC.

There was a conjunction of planets that could have provided the guiding light. A conjunction occurs when two objects appear to come close together. This occurs when both objects have the same celestial longitude. In 3 BC and 2 BC, there was a series of close conjunctions involving Jupiter, the planet that represented kingship and the birth of kings. In Hebrew, Jupiter was known as *Sedeq* or Righteousness, a term used for the Messiah.

In September 3 BC, Jupiter came into conjunction with Regulus, the star of kingship, the brightest star in the constellation of Leo. Leo was associated with the Lion of Judah. The royal planet approached the royal star in the royal constellation representing Israel. A month earlier Jupiter and Venus, the Mother planet, seemed to almost touch each other. Such a heavenly display could not have been missed by the Wise Men.

Such is one explanation of the Star of Bethlehem. It may never be known for sure exactly how the star is explained.

THE PLACE OF JESUS' BIRTH

Hospitality was the norm in Israel at the time of Jesus' birth. Seventy-six verses in the Old Testament refer to hospitality. Mary and Joseph had relatives in Bethlehem. The culture of the time would have caused the local relatives to welcome a cousin, especially one who was a descendant of a king, specifically King David. To have turned away such a relative would have been insulting to both parties. To establish one's heritage necessitated only reciting four of five generations, which Mary and Joseph could have done.

The Greek word describing their housing is *kataluma* and can be translated variously as living area, guest room, hostel, upper room, or tent. From this comes the word *inn*. It is the same word as used for the place Jesus observed the Last Supper with the apostles. The Greek word for a commercial inn is *pandokeion* and is not used regarding the birth narrative.

Thus applied, the word could mean there was no room in the regular family living quarters. Therefore, relatives allowed them to settle where the cattle were in their cave. People still live in caves in a region near Bethlehem south of Hebron.

Normally, animals were stalled in a portion of the cave separated from the humans by thorny branches. Occasionally, there were two caves, one above the other, with an opening between them. The animals helped provide heat for the people. In addition to providing shelter for the birth, the cave also would have allowed privacy. There being no room in the living quarters, Mary would have given birth in the cave, but not in the living quarters of it. This would have been in keeping with the customs of the time and practices by the Bedouins today.

From the first century, a certain cave in Bethlehem has been venerated as the place of the birth.

Secular sources contain this first century reference to such a cave: "Under the tumbled ruins of Chimham's famous khan at the edge of town was a stable-cave where Bethlehemites believe Jesus was born."

Jeremiah 41: 17 refers to such a place, saying Jews under the command of Johanan who, fleeing from the Babylonians, "dwelt in the habitation of Chimham, which is by Bethlehem."

Magi, Wise Men, would soon make their way to see the newborn king. Magi were priests who were the teachers of the Persian kings in matters of philosophy and science. They were actually members of a priestly tribe among the Medes. Daniel in his prophetic text mentions Magi four times. They were not kings, but king- makers. One of their principal roles was the selection of their king. Their experience stimulated their interest in one "born king of the Jews."

Their homeland was about a thousand miles directly east of Bethlehem. Their traveling routes would have been between twelve hundred and fifteen hundred miles. If they had averaged twenty-five miles a day, the journey would have required approximately fifty days. Such a journey would have required them to form a large caravan to transport food for their animals, themselves, their servants, and guards. Transporting valuable gifts would have required security.

No self-respecting Magi would have ridden a camel. That would have been like an eighteen-wheeler and beneath the dignity of their office. They would not have used horses because Romans used them. Donkeys were not capable of such a journey. They would have ridden mules.

These royal guests were not kings. Had they been kings, Herod would have kept the custom of the day and welcomed them with a feast. Instead, he ordered them to go and bring back a report on what they found.

Daniel, who was exiled in Babylon long before, became a Magi. He would have been their source of insight regarding a star and royal birth.

To avoid the desert heat, they would have traveled at night. As an aside, that made it easy to follow the star. Scripture notes they saw the star in the east. It was they who were in the east. Bethlehem was west from them, and the star would have been to their west; thus, it was actually a western, not an eastern, star.

A church, Saint Helena, was the first built over the traditional site of Jesus' birth in 339. After a fire in the sixth century, the present Church of the Nativity replaced it in 533.

The masterful mosaics inside the church are believed to be from the tenth century.

One of the colorful mosaics was responsible for the church being spared when the Persians invaded the area in 614 and destroyed most churches. A beautiful mosaic over the main entrance of the church depicted the three Wise Men as clad in Persian attire. Thus, they spared the church.

Today to enter the church, one must bow to go through the entrance. Around the year fifteen hundred, marauders would ride their horses and carts into the church and loot it. To prevent this, villagers enclosed the original entrance one night, making it slightly less than four feet tall.

To pilgrims, it seems appropriate to bow before entering the place of Christ's birth.

The building has various portions governed by different Christian faiths. The main basilica is mostly Greek Orthodox. To the right of the main altar are steps leading down into the Grotto of the Birth which is controlled by the Greek Orthodox Church. This portion of the cave beneath the altar is revered as the place of Jesus' birth. A fourteen-point star on the marble floor bears the inscription, *Hic de Virgine Maria Jesus Christus natus,* meaning Here Jesus Christ was born of the Virgin Mary.

The Grotto of the Manger commemorates the visit by the Wise Men. It is larger than a feeding trough. A small altar in the Grotto of the Manger dedicated to the oration of the Magi is where Roman Catholics celebrate Mass.

Tapestries line the walls, and ornate oil lamps hang from the ceiling. All are gifts of heads of state and notable individuals from all over the world who have visited there through the ages. They cover the walls which are stained by fires from years ago.

Jesus would likely have been three years old when the Wise Men came. The Greek word for baby, or infant is *brephos*. The Greek word *paidion*, which is used in reference to the child when the Wise Men visited, is translated young child (Matthew 2: 11). The fact Herod ordered the execution of all male children in Bethlehem under the age of three is also an indication Jesus was likely older when visited by the Wise Men.

Visitors find it to be a moving moment to stand there and think, "Here, right here, the Word became flesh and came and dwelt among us." Immanuel had arrived on planet earth; the God who was for us was now with us. While man was trying to make himself a god, God made Himself a man.

JESUS' EDUCATION

Jesus Christ was Immanuel, God with us. He was as much human as though He were not God and as much God as though He were not man. He was the God/man-man/God.

He was God with a heartbeat, a tint to His eyes, and red blood coursing through His veins. He was also God incarnate, that is, inhabiting a human form. To align these two natures, He is depicted as having "emptied Himself." Thus, He never used His divine nature for His own welfare, though He often did for others.

Without using His divine nature for Himself, He had to learn and develop as a human being. That means He had to learn languages like anyone else. Above Him on the cross was the inscription written in Latin, Greek, and Hebrew. These were the principal languages of the day, along with Aramaic.

Aramaic had been spoken there since the return from the Babylonian exile.

During all of his conquests, Alexander the Great required people in the conquered regions to speak Greek. The diaspora involved dispersing Jews throughout the Hellenistic world. A long list of diverse areas into which they were spread is found in Acts 2: 9-11. Babylon, Rome, and Alexandria had large Jewish colonies. Jews returning from those areas after the diaspora would have returned speaking Greek.

Hebrew was the language in which the Old Testament texts were written. However, Hebrew was not used in everyday life since the second century. It was only used in the synagogue as a prayer language. The more educated people knew Greek. It was the lingua franca all over the eastern part of the Roman Empire.

Greek was spoken in the Greek/Roman cities of Sepphoris and Beit She'an and in the cities of the Decapolis which Jesus visited on two occasions. The Decapolis (ten cities) were Greek cities mostly east of the Jordan River. They were developed by Greek settler-soldiers of the Ptolemaic and Selecuid kingdoms. The Jews referred to the region as the other side, with reference to the Sea of Galilee. Gergesenes, modern Kursi, was in the area of the Decapolis. In this area Jesus fed the four thousand, not to be confused with the feeding of the five thousand. It was in this region Jesus cast the swine out of the demon-possessed man. In general, people in the region would not have spoken Aramaic or Hebrew. People from the Decapolis are said to have followed Jesus. This indicated they understood His speech on many occasions.

Pilate, being Roman, would have had Latin as his primary language. Greek, rather than Aramaic or Hebrew, would have been his second language. This would have well suited him for work in the courts which were conducted in Greek.

It is estimated by some scholars that 20 percent of the people in Jerusalem spoke Greek.

If Jesus spoke Greek, He had to learn it as any other youth. That raises the question of when and how He learned it. Logically, He would not have learned it in Nazareth.

Nearby, less than four miles and visible from Nazareth, was the thriving, sophisticated Greek-founded city of Sepphoris. In many translations of Scripture, the word *carpenter* is used to describe Joseph's occupation. The text could better be translated *craftsman*, which, of course, allows for it also being translated carpenter. However, it can also be translated stonemason. There are no trees around Nazareth and no need for a carpenter in Nazareth. Seeking work and engaging in commerce, it is logical that Joseph would have visited the bustling city of Sepphoris often. It would not have been uncommon for the young Jesus to have accompanied him. Sons of tradesmen often followed their fathers as apprentices.

Today, as in that era, it is not uncommon in parts of the world that when a family of means encounters a less fortunate family with an obviously gifted child, the affluent family offers to take the child and see that he is educated. The following scenario is possibly how Jesus came to know Greek. Such a family could have taken the young boy Jesus and seen to it He was educated. This would not only account for how He learned Greek, but finance and commerce also.

The following is the basis for that conjecture: "Joanna, the wife of Chuza, Herod's steward, and Susanna, and many others who provided for them out of their resources" (Luke 8:3). Herod Antipas, the son of Herod the Great, had become ruler of Galilee and east of the Jordan. Chuza, being in such a strategic office, would have been a very wealthy man. Women of that time were not allowed to have money of their own, so Joanna would have had access to the wealth of Chuza.

The faith of Joanna must have been shared by Chuza. If so, it was at great risk. It was his boss, Herod Antipas, who had beheaded John the Baptist. Herod would not have been pleased to know the wife of one of his officials was so kindly disposed toward Jesus. Perhaps it was Chuza's fond memories of the boy Jesus that inspired him.

The women, having followed Jesus and the apostles, were present at the crucifixion (Luke 23: 49). They even followed Joseph of

Arimathea to the tomb (Luke 23: 55). Once the Sabbath was over, they came to the tomb in the early morning. A sidebar truth to the angel's announcement regarding the Resurrection is that the messenger said, "Remember how He spoke to you" and "they remembered" (Luke 24: 6 & 8). Contrary to the custom of the time, Jesus had obviously taught not only His disciples, but also the women. Mary and Martha are examples of this.

This concept is supposition, but it offers insight into how Jesus might have become well educated.

JESUS' BAPTISM

Ritual immersion in water was a well-established religious cleansing ritual. Baptism was intended to symbolize cleansing from sin as well as an initiation rite into an order. In the instance of Jesus' baptism by John, it was His identification with those who would follow after Him. Jesus endorsed baptism at the time of conversion "in the name of the Father, the Son, and the Holy Spirit."

Immersion for spiritual cleansing was essential before entering the temple or participating in festivals. *Mikveh*, or ritual baths, have been found all over the country. In the New Testament it was considered a meaningful act of identity with Jesus' death, burial, and resurrection.

The word *baptisma* has been anglicized to mean immersing or pouring rather than being properly translated to mean *immersion*. Texts such as the following strongly favor it being translated *immersion*: Acts 2: 38-41; 8: 26-39; 9:17, 18; 22: 12-16; 10: 44-48; 16: 32-34.

For baptism to symbolize cleansing in the Christian community, as it did in the Jewish community, it necessitated immersion, which was the norm among Christians until around circa 300.

TOPOGRAPHY

The State of Israel consists of 8,630 square miles. It is two hundred and ninety miles long and about eighty-five miles wide at the widest point. Lebanon, Syria, Jordan, and Egypt are its neighbors. To drive east to west at its widest point takes about ninety minutes, from north to south about six hours.

The diverse topography of the land lends itself to a variety of environments appealing to different cultures.

By natural formations, Israel divides itself into distinct regions. For such a small country to have such distinct terrain and climate is unusual:

- The Mediterranean Sea affords an outlet to other more western cultures.
- The Coastal Plain runs along the Mediterranean Sea from Lebanon in the north to Gaza in the south. This fertile and humid region is twenty miles in width at its widest part. It is the home of more than half of the country's population.
- The Central Highlands is a ridge rising precipitously a short distance inland. It consists of the Upper and Lower Galilee Mountains, and further south, the Samarian Hills. Mount Hermon with a height of 7,336 feet is the highest point in Israel. The most prominent valley crossing the range is the Jezreel Valley also known as the Plain of Esdraelon.
- The Great Rift Valley, through which the Jordan River flows, runs from Syria in the north to East Africa in the south.
- The Jordan River begins near the northern end of the Rift Valley. The river results from the convergence of water from the Dan, Banyas, and Hasbany Springs, which get their water primarily from Mount Hermon. Flowing north to south through the rift, it descends over twenty-three hundred feet in its course of one hundred and eighty-six miles.
- The Transjordan Highlands begins on the east bank of the Jordan River. Syria and Jordan constitute this region.

- The Sea of Galilee is near the base of Mount Hermon, out of which the Jordan River flows.
- The Dead Sea is the southern terminal of the Jordan River.

Five of these distinct terrains run parallel the length of the country.

The Negev Desert, which is basically independent of these delineations, constitutes more than half of Israel. Geographically it is an extension of the Sinai Desert. And Israel hosts the lowest spot on earth, the Dead Sea, which is 1,368 feet below sea level. Nearby is the lowest city on earth, Jericho.

Many of the sites of tels that have played a major role in the history of the land were cities destroyed by earthquakes, fires, and age. The cities of Capernaum, Corazine, Beit She'an, and Hippos are examples of cities destroyed by earthquakes. Being in the Great Rift Valley that runs from Africa into Europe, the country is ideally located for geological upheavals. Since 31 BC, there have been thirty-seven major quakes in the country with the worst being in 31 BC, 363, 749, and 1033:

- Josephus wrote that the 31 BC quake resulted in thirty thousand fatalities.
- In the quake of 1068, more than twenty thousand died.
- In 1038, an earthquake lasted forty days.

Some of these quakes completely destroyed major cities. Hippos on the Golan is an example. So complete was the devastation of this large, lovely city that inhabitants simply abandoned it. The massive remains of large stone buildings are a testimony to the severity of the earthquake. Such earthquakes have contributed to tel development.

THE TALE OF A TEL

Tel is an archaeological term referring to a place inhabited by humans over an extended period of time. Tels have distinctive reasons for their place of development. For commercial reasons, many were on or near trade routes. Some locations were based on the position being defensible. This necessitated the position being elevated, whether naturally or by human efforts. The availability of water was always an expedient.

Some modern cities in Israel have developed from once-small tels. Many such cities have "tel" in their name.

Cities were most often built on an elevation which was fortified, having high walls, gates, and adequate water supply. Outside the city were settlements of people who were engaged in agriculture or a trade needing space. When an enemy approached, they could retreat within the defensible city walls.

Walls of most of these were made of mud bricks and/or larger stones gathered from the area. Victorious invaders often completely destroyed a conquered city after sacking and pillaging it. Most often that included tearing down buildings and some, if not all, of the city walls.

A subsequent society would often choose to build on the same site because it was in a good location, had water, and held some residual building material. The mud bricks would eventually erode and add to the elevation of the site. New developers would level the site and build on the rubble of the previous city. Over the centuries, this was done as many as twenty times in some cities. This could result in a significant buildup. Also, if there were people who had lived in the demolished city, they could reclaim their property on which to build.

Archaeologists often slice the tel like a cake, removing a segment like layers of a cake and exposing the entire tel. By examining artifacts such as coins, pottery, tools, or stone, they can read the layers like a book. This reveals the time and history of the culture. Excavations at Megiddo reveal there have been twenty-six different cultures to inhabit the tel.

Tels were developed between the fifth and third centuries BC. Tels died out for a number of reasons, one being the extent of military destruction and annihilation of the inhabitants. Some grew too large, and the citizens rebuilt in nearby elevated locations, often even more defendable. When this was done, a remnant often used the old location as an outpost for farmers or as a military garrison.

Beit She'an is a classic example. The first settlement there was built during the Chalcolithic period. Over the centuries, it was destroyed and rebuilt many times, resulting in an enormous tel today. After the last settlement, citizens built a large, opulent city nearby. Remains of that city are more exposed and reveal a very progressive culture. Built around those ruins is the current city of Beit She'an.

There are over two hundred tels in Israel. Several are parks in modern Israel. Three tels, Hazor, Megiddo, and Beersheba, are classic tels attracting numerous visitors. Beersheba is an example of an abandoned city. For nearly two thousand years, it was uninhabited. Because of its strategic location on trade routes, it was rebuilt as a planned city, not one that grew in stages over time.

PALESTINE

Palestine is a geographic region in Western Asia. It is generally defined as a territory in the Southern Levant between the Mediterranean Sea and the Jordan River and joining lands. Until 1948, all who lived in this region were called Palestinians, including Jews and Arabs.

The word *Palestine* was derived from *Philisia*, the Greek name for the land of the Philistines who ruled a small territory between present-day Tel Aviv and Gaza. The Romans applied it to the southern portion of Syria. Eventually, the Islamic people began to use it to refer to the entire region.

Both the geographic area designated by the name and the political status of it have changed over approximately three thousand years.

As names like Baltic and North America speak of regions, not independent states, so Palestine was a reference to a region ruled by various cultures over the years. Consequently, with the passing of time, the occupants of the region became an amalgam of societies such as, but not limited to, the Canaanites, Amorites, Egyptians, Moabites, Ammonites, Philistines, Assyrians, Babylonians, Persians, ancient Greeks, Romans and Brzabtines.

In 1947, the newly formed United Nations partitioned the region of Palestine into two zones, Israel for the Jews and Palestine for the Arabs. From these bodies have emerged Israel and a self-governing society named Palestine. Palestine as a nation did not exist prior until 1947.

A timeline showing Israel dwelling in the land follows:

- 1120 BC—The Israelite army led by Barak and Deborah defeated the Canaanite armies of Sisera at the battle at Mount Tabor.
- 1026 BC—Saul became the first king of Israel.
- 1004 BC—Ish-bosheth became the second king of Israel.
- 1003 BC—David became the third king of what became known as the United Kingdom of Israel.

Prior to this, "The Lord made a covenant with Abram saying, 'To your descendants I have given this land, from the river of Egypt to the great river, the River Euphrates'" (Genesis 15: 18). As Abraham journeyed into the land, "The Lord appeared to Abram and said, 'To your descendants I will give this land'" (Genesis 12: 7).

The Hebrew word translated *give* is used to describe God bequeathing the land to Abraham. It is translated by sixty-three different words such as *assign*, *ascribe*, and bestow, making it all the more an emphatic act.

Not without reason did God give the land of the Canaanites to Abraham and his descendants. Moses told the children of Abraham God was taking the land from the Canaanites: "Because of the wickedness of these nations the Lord God drives them out before you" (Deuteronomy 9: 5).

Just before Moses' death, God took him up on Mount Pisgah and showed him the land of promise saying, "This is the land which I swore to give to Abraham, Isaac, and Jacob, saying, 'I will give it to your descendants'" (Deuteronomy 34: 4).

JERUSALEM

Great is the Lord, and greatly to be praised

In the city of our God, In His holy mountain.

Beautiful in elevation, The joy of the whole earth,

Is Mount Zion on the sides of the north,

The city of the great King.   ~ Psalm 48: 1, 2

DESTRUCTION OF JERUSALEM

Jerusalem has been attacked fifty-two times, captured and recaptured forty-four times, besieged twenty-three times, and destroyed twice. Older parts of the city were settled in the fourth millennium BC.

In these conflicts, the city has been partially destroyed four times. The first was around 1400 BC when captured by the tribes of Judah and Simeon, the second in 586 BC by Nebuchadnezzar, the third in 170 BC by Antiochus Epiphanies, and the fourth and most horrendous in 70 by the Roman General Titus. The city was restored by Hadrian but has been fought over several times since.

The destruction which occurred shortly after the New Testament era in 70 was a final engagement in the battle of the Jews against the Romans.

Jesus spoke of the "abomination of desolation" (Matthew 24: 15, 16), literally the abomination which leads to desecration. It was a reference to the abomination leading to the desecration of the Temple. The Roman siege led to abominable actions among the besieged, panicky people whose conduct in the Temple defamed it, making its inevitable end near. Jesus warned of such a destructive siege, telling believers to flee the city when they saw it surrounded.

The Roman army under the command of the General Vespasian consisted of thirty thousand warriors, and the Jewish army numbered twenty-four thousand. In addition to the normal population of Jerusalem, there were six hundred thousand visitors from Egypt to Babylon who had crowded into the city for the Passover. The Romans built earthen redoubts and put battering rams in place as the siege began. Persons attempting to escape were crucified within view of persons in the city. The historian Josephus notes there were more than a million Jewish casualties and ninety-seven thousand captives taken into slavery during the Roman War.

General Vespasian had the city completely cut off when one morning the people of the city awoke to find the Roman army had withdrawn. Roman Emperor Nero had died, and Vespasian had gone to Rome to contend to become emperor.

Remembering the warning of Jesus regarding fleeing upon seeing the city surrounded, Christians left the city in large numbers and went to Pella upon seeing the withdrawal.

Later fear once more swept through the city when the Roman 10th Legions under the command of General Titus arrived at the outermost northern wall of Jerusalem.

The siege lasted five months. Starvation and infighting within factions in the city greatly depleted Jewish capacity to survive. Hunger was so rampant cannibalism resulted.

Finally, the walls of the city were breached, the Temple was decimated, and the city was left in ruins, desolate. Herod's three great towers at the northwest corner of the city remained and served as a memorial of the strength of the fortifications of the once-proud city which lay in rubble.

A second major revolt which occurred in 135 was led by Bar Kokhba. The emperor Hadrian suppressed it and totally rebuilt Jerusalem.

THE GATES OF JERUSALEM

The beautiful walls of the Old City of Jerusalem contain eight gates, seven of which are open for public use. They are Herod's Gate, Damascus Gate, New Gate, Jaffa Gate, Zion Gate, Dung Gate, Eastern Gate, and Lions' Gate.

THE EAST GATE

The Eastern Gate is also known as the Golden Gate and considered by some to be the Gate Beautiful. Today it is sealed. Two possible dates of the sealing are suggested. Perhaps it was closed for security reasons during the numerous Arab-Crusader clashes from the eleventh to the thirteenth centuries or perhaps after Suleiman the Magnificent rebuilt the walls from 1539 to 1542. The gate was refurbished by the Turkish authorities in 1891.

The valley outside the gate is known as the Kedron Valley and the Valley of Jehosaphat. Though it bears the name of King Jehoshaphat, it is the meaning of the word that gives it spiritual significance. It means judgment, giving the gate the name of the Judgment Gate.

The prophet Joel spoke of there being judgment at the site: "And I will show wonders in the heavens and in the earth: blood and fire and pillars of smoke. The sun shall be turned into darkness, and the moon into blood, before the coming of the great day of the Lord" (Joel 2: 30 - 31).

Assuming the Eastern Gate to be the site of this judgment, Jews and Muslims desire to be among the first to rise on resurrection morning. Therefore, they desire to be buried a close to the gate as possible.

Golden Gate is a name given the gate by Christians. The New Testament makes reference to the Beautiful Gate (Acts 3: 1, 10). The word *beautiful* may have evolved from a translation by Jerome of the Greek word *oraia* into the Latin sounding word *aurea*, meaning golden.

A gate beneath the present visible gate was accidentally discovered in April of 1969 when an explorer fell into a grave near the present gate and found himself facing an ancient subterranean gate. It was almost immediately sealed off. However, photographs and personal details provided give clues to its age.

Most scholars date the adjacent masonry to a time prior to Hadrian, indicating it is ancient. Exactly how old it is has not been determined, but a date as early as the time of Solomon is acknowledged to be possible. If so, it would likely have been an esteemed gate though the ages. It is considered highly probable that this subsurface gate was the gate through which Jesus entered Jerusalem.

THE LIONS' GATE

Facing the Eastern Gate, the first gate to the right is the Lions' Gate. Today it also known as St. Stephen's Gate, the only open gate facing east. It was part of the construction by the Ottoman Sultan Suleiman the Magnificent when he rebuilt the walls of the city in the sixteenth century.

A stone lion is located on each side of the gate, giving the area the name, which stands for Jerusalem and Judah. However, the lions were originally put there by the Ottomans in honor of Mameluke Sultan Bybars, known as the Lion of Egypt and Syria.

The outside road leads down through the Kidon Valley, over the Mount of Olives to Jericho. Inside the wall, the street soon becomes part of the Via Dolorosa, the Way of the Cross.

Immediately inside the gate on the right is Saint Ann's Church, which according to a Crusader's tradition based on an Apocryphal book, is believed to have been the site of the birth of the virgin Mary. Hence, the gate is also called St. Mary's Gate. It is known as Saint Stephen's Gate in honor of the first Christian martyr believed to have been killed there.

Above the gate a terrace stands out from which boiling oil could be poured on would-be invaders in ancient times.

It is one of the gates through which Jewish Israeli Defense Forces entered Jerusalem during the Six-day War in 1967.

HEROD'S GATE

Herod's Gate, which dates from the Crusader period, is in the northern wall of Jerusalem, a short distance from the Damascus Gate and provides entrance into the Muslim Quarter. The floral design above the gate has earned it the name of the Flowers Gate. It is known principally as Herod's Gate, because nearby Crusaders found impressive ruins they improperly thought to be Herod's palace. Herod's palace was actually on the most western hill near the Jaffa Gate. A few yards from the present gate is where the Crusaders breached the wall in their conquest of the city.

DAMASCUS GATE

This is the most imposing of all the gates and one of the busiest. Facing north, it is named for the city to which it leads, Damascus.

When the Romans conquered Jerusalem in 70, they destroyed most of the city. In 130 Emperor Hadrian rebuilt the city, naming it Aelia Capitolina.

When Suleiman the Magnificent rebuilt the walls of Jerusalem in the sixteenth century, he completely covered the previous entryway. Above the previous gate, he built the most magnificent gate, the Damascus Gate. Beyond the entrance, the previous gate built by Hadrian can be seen to the left and below. Also, to be seen are the remains of a prior gate attributed to Agrippa. This gives an idea of how much lower the previous entrance was.

During the Byzantine period, it was called St. Stephens Gate because of its proximity to St. Stephens Church, one of the reputed sites of the martyrdom of Saint Stephen. It should be noted that two gates are called Saint Stephens. The title is given them at different times.

Presently, it is the entrance to one of the most bustling markets.

NEW GATE

The New Gate is the newest gate, having been built by Sultan Abdul Hamid II in 1889 near the northwestern corner of the city. It is the only gate not included in the original design of the sixteenth century wall. It is the primary entrance into the Christian Quarter.

JAFFA GATE

The gate received its name from the city to which pilgrims exiting traveled, Jaffa.

Immediately inside the gate is the Tower of David and the imposing market. The second street to the left after entering leads a short distance to a Roman stele, which was a mile marker indicating a camp of the 10th Roman Legion.

In 1898, the controlling Ottoman authorities opened the old wall next to the older Jaffa Gate so the German Kaiser Wilhelm II and his wife could enter on horseback along with their escort. It was the first gate opened to automobiles. His coming established a strong German presence and enlarged the influence of the Lutheran church in Jerusalem.

Immediately to the left of this larger gate is the earlier L-shaped Jaffa Gate built in 1538 under Ottoman rule. It was so shaped to put an invader at a disadvantage having to turn the corners.

The Citadel, also known as the Tower of David, is in the quarter near the Jaffa Gate. It was built on the highest point in the Old City, including the Temple Mount. It stands on the ruins of fortifications from the end of the monarchic period, the sixth to the eighth century. The Citadel itself was built in the mid-sixteenth century and incorporates the remains of a previous Citadel that stood on the site. Though it has been destroyed and rebuilt many times, sixteen courses of the original tower still form the base.

The adjacent Tower of David Museum, in addition to housing numerous historical artifacts, is itself a historical site worth exploring. The tower and courtyard are a popular venue for the sound-and-light show as well as art exhibits.

It is regarded as the site at which King Herod greeted the Wise Men who came seeking Jesus.

In 132, Hadrian conquered the city and renamed it Aelia Capitoline and began reconstruction. As part of the development, he had constructed a tall pillar inside the gate to be used as the starting point for measuring distances to and from the city.

Currently one of the busiest streets begins at the plaza inside the gate. It forks with the street straight ahead leading to the Jewish Quarter and the fork to the right to the Armenian Quarter.

ZION GATE

Located in the south, it was built to afford entrance to the Armenian and Jewish Quarters. It was so named because it faced Mount Zion. It is also known as the Gate of the Jews and David's Gate. It was one of the L-shaped gates, designed for security reasons. Like other gates, it had openings above the entrance allowing for boiling oil to be poured on would-be invaders. It was sealed from 1948 to 1967. It was one of the primary gates through which the Israeli Defense Fighters, the IDF, entered the city in the Six-day War. It leads to both the Jewish and Armenian Quarters.

DUNG GATE

Located in the southern wall, it is the gate closest to the Temple Mount. It was the principal gate through which refuse of the city was taken out in olden times, hence the name Dung Gate. Ash and garbage from the temple were disposed of through this gate also.

Imbued with such a lowly name initially, it now is the most convenient gate to the Western Wall. It is one of only four gates providing for vehicles.

QUARTERS OF JERUSALEM

Until 1860, there were no developed areas immediately outside the walls of the Old City. The gates continued to be closed at night long after that.

The Old City of Jerusalem which covers two hundred and twenty acres, approximately one square mile, is divided into four primary quarters: Christian, Jewish, Muslim, and Armenian. They not only divide the city geographically, but politically, socially, culturally, and religiously. They form a rectangular grid of different sizes. The street that runs from Damascus Gate to Zion Gate divides the city east and west. The street running from Jaffa Gate to Lions' Gate divides the city north and south.

The Jewish Quarter is located on the remains of the upper city from the Herodian era, 37 BC to 70. The quarter is accessed from outside the city through the Dung Gate just outside the Western Wall and the Zion Gate.

This section, located on the southwest side of the Old City, began to emerge as the Jewish Quarter in the thirteenth century following the Crusades. However, habitation began when the walls of Jerusalem were extended westward by Hezekiah in the eighth century BC. It is believed the first residents were fleeing Senacherib's military campaign. Remains of Hezekiah's Wall, known as the Broad Wall are visible on Plugot Hakotel Street.

The paramount feature of the quarter is the Western Wall. This is the only section of the wall remaining from the Roman destruction of the city in 70. It was not part of the Temple but was part of the outer wall that surrounded the Temple Mount. It is perhaps the most highly venerated place in Jewish society. The lower part of the wall has been discovered all the way to the Fortress

Antonia.

The Cardo, which dates from the time of Hadrian as 135, was approximately the size of an eight-lane highway and ran north and south in the quarter. It was the main street of Jerusalem fifteen hundred years ago. A section of the old road has been excavated exposing the impressive ruins of the stores that lined the colonnade.

The Armenian Quarter is located in the southwestern corner of the Old City and is accessed from without through the Jaffa and Zion gates. It is separated from the Christian Quarter by David Street and from the Jewish Quarter by Habad Street.

In 301, Armenia officially adopted Christianity as its national religion. Thereafter, Armenian monks began to move into Jerusalem and settled what is now the Armenian Quarter.

Though officially separated from the Greek Orthodox and Catholic Christians, they consider themselves part of the Christian community. The population of the quarter has been diminishing for some time.

Herod built a fort and his imposing palace on the grounds just south of the modern bastion Tower of David. The development included three towers named for his wife Mariamne, his friend Hippicus, and his brother Phasael. It is the last of these that is still standing.

The Christian Quarter is located in the northwest corner of the Old City. It extends from the New Gate in the north to the Damascus Gate in the east where it borders the Muslim Quarter. Numbered among the forty Christian sights in the quarter is the Church of the Holy Sepulcher.

In the nineteenth century, European countries built several facilities in the quarter. An influx of tourists motivated the French to develop an area outside the city walls known as the French area. The Russians did also. To permit commerce between the Christian Quarter and the French, a new gate was opened in the city walls known as the New Gate.

The Via Dolorosa winds its way through the quarter to the Church of the Holy Sepulcher.

A colorful thriving market place near the Church of the Holy Sepulcher was also a large courtyard during the Roman era. During the Crusader era, knights known as the Hospitallers resided here and built two churches, Santa Maria Grande and Santa Maria Latina.

The Muslim Quarter is located in the northeast corner of the Old City. It is the largest and most heavily populated quarter, including nearly two thirds of the population of the city. It extends from the Lions' Gate in the east to the Damascus Gate in the west. The first seven Stations of the Cross are in the quarter as are a number of Roman and Crusader landmarks.

The area was first settled at the end of the Second Temple period and was included within the second wall built by Herod the Great.

Due to ethnic differences nearly two thousand years ago, during the seven-hundred-year Mameluke period which followed the expulsion of the Crusaders, it became known as the Muslim Quarter. The quarter is accessed from outside the city through the Lions' Gate, Herod's Gate, and Damascus Gate. The Temple Mount where the Al-Aqsa Mosque now stands is in the southern edge of the quarter. This thirty-five-acre compound is known as the Noble Sanctuary by Muslims and the Temple Mount by Jews.

There are several buildings on the grounds in addition to the mosque. The most prominent is the golden-domed shrine known as the Dome of the Rock. Contrary to the common concept that it is a mosque, it is not; it is a shrine.

WESTERN WAILING WALL

When the Romans destroyed the Temple and most of the walls of the city in 70, the Western Wall was considered of so little significance they allowed it to stand. It was, after all, not a part of the Temple. It was only an outer wall of the Temple Mount.

It was given the name the Wailing Wall during the time the Jews were exiled from the land and could return only once a year to mourn the destruction of the Temple.

During the thousand-year Muslim rule, as a show of indignity, Muslims used the area as a trash dump.

The Western Wall of the Temple Mount is called the *Kotel*, meaning The Wall. The Romans destroyed the upper part of the Western Wall by pushing the stones from the upper level outward. The falling stones buried the lower levels. In a more recent time, fallen stones were removed exposing the portion of the wall known as the Wailing Wall. Believing this to be the closest they could come to the Temple Mount, Jews removed the stones to gather there for prayer.

KOTEL TUNNEL

Adjacent to the Western Wall on the left is a tunnel exposing a part of the wall not visible above ground. The exposed portion of the Western Wall is approximately two hundred feet, while this underground section is 1,591 feet. Much of the tunnel runs under present-day Muslim residences. The tunnel begins at the Western Wall and ends at the Via Dolorosa.

Near the entrance is what is believed to be one of the heaviest and largest objects to have ever been moved without mechanical means. This stone, known as the Western Stone, measures forty-five feet in length and nine feet in height, weighing five hundred and twenty metric tons.

About midway through the tunnel is a sealed gate which is the closest point to the original Holy of Holies. Here Jews enjoy praying because of the proximity to the Temple Mount.

At the northern part of the tunnel are the remains of a water tunnel which supplied water to the Temple Mount. Here also is exposed a portion of the enormous stone on which a part of the Temple Mount stands. It is carved to give it the appearance of the cut stones that constitute the wall.

EASTERN TEMPLE MOUNT WALL

In order to have a plateau on which to build the Temple and his royal palace, around 960 BC Solomon built massive retaining walls, like a box, and filled the area within to create a level platform for the imposing buildings. The Temple Mount, as it is known today, is an artificial earthen podium.

In 587 BC, the Babylonians led by Nebuchnezzar destroyed Jerusalem including the Solomonic Temple.

In the first century BC, Herod the Great basically rebuilt the Temple. It was destroyed by the Romans in 70. Herod extended the line of Solomon's wall north, south, and west, doubling the size of the Solomonic Temple Mount. With rare exception, the original walls are buried underground within the present walls of the current city.

Most of the visible walls of today were built by the Ottoman Emperor Sultan Suleiman between 1537 and 1541.

On the eastern side of Jerusalem, Solomon built the retaining wall on the steep slope going down into the Kidron Valley. Herod extended this eastern wall to the north and south. Approximately a hundred feet from the southeastern corner of the Temple Mount, there is a straight line in the masonry wall. Normally blocks are spaced alternately one on top to the other giving support to joints. This straight line reveals where the old and new walls met. The line is clearly visible on the lower thirty-eight feet of the wall.

Understandably, the Western Wall attracts the most attention, but the Eastern Wall predates it.

THE HERODIAN STREET

In 70, the Roman Legions under the leadership of Titus, son of Emperor Vespasian, overran and pillaged Jerusalem, leaving most of its walls in ruins. To the right of the Western Wall and running to the southwest corner of the Herodian Temple Mount is Herodian Street which dates to the time of Jesus.

It traces the Tyropoeon Valley which separates the wall and the western hills of the Upper City. The street was composed of thick, smooth stones which made it easy for walking. Small shops lined the street.

High up on the wall the remains of a massive arch projects from the western wall known as Robinson's Arch. It was once a primary entrance into the Temple Mount.

Among the large stones pushed down by the Romans is a cornerstone with the Hebrew inscription *To the trumpeting place*.... The most likely missing portion would have read *proclaim*. It would have been the southwestern corner of the Temple Mount where the trumpeter stood to make instrumental pronouncements.

Visitors can walk this street with confidence that they are walking where Jesus walked in the days this was a bustling thoroughfare.

SOUTHERN TEMPLE MOUNT WALL

Along the southern wall of the Temple Mount are stairs consisting of fifteen alternating wide and narrow steps. It is suggested the fifteen long steps may have been one of the locations where pilgrims paused and sang the fifteen Psalms of Ascent (Psalm 120 - 134).

The Double Gates and Triple Gates, also known as the Hulda Gate, which were two hundred and thirty feet apart, provided entrance to the Temple Mount through a subterranean passageway. The pilgrims' road from the Pool of Siloam to the Temple Mount led through these gates.

The Triple Gates, now sealed, were a total of fifty-one feet wide. Each gate was thirteen feet wide with two six-foot piers separating them. There is debate as to whether this or the Eastern Gate is considered to be the Beautiful Gate (Acts 3: 2).

The Double Gate led to the Temple Mount through an ornate tunnel beneath the Royal Stoa on the southern end of Solomon's Colonnade. Here, a stairway enabled worshipers to ascend to the outer courtyard of the Temple Mount. The distance from the street level to the Double Gate up the stairs to the Temple Mount surface was about forty-six feet.

Ritual purification laws necessitated a number of public ritual baths known as *mikvah*. Large ritual *mikvah* baths had a small dividing wall to separate persons entering and those exiting.

These mikvah were doubtlessly used by Peter on the Day of Pentecost when three thousand new converts were baptized.

Peter and John, on their way to pray one afternoon, met a crippled man here at the Gate Beautiful. He was being carried there, as was the custom, to beg for money. He went with them into the Temple courts. Upon being healed, he started walking, jumping, and praising God. And "all the people were astonished and came running to them in the place called Solomon's Colonnade" (Acts 3: 1 - 11).

TEMPLE MOUNT

The Temple Mount is an artificial, elevated plaza built within the casement of the surrounding walls. Both of Israel's former temples stood here. It is also the third holiest place in Islam. At present, the site is under Israeli sovereignty, but is ministered by the Muslin Waqf (a religious trust). These circumstances make it a place of frequent interreligious conflict.

Tradition holds that it is the site where Abraham offered to sacrifice his son Isaac.

The present Temple Mount is a thirty-five-acre artificial plaza, the construction of which began in 20 BC by Herod the Great and continued for eighty-three years until 64 when eighteen thousand workers were laid off, causing riots. The project made the summit of the mount a level court. Below the present plaza are nineteen additional courses of Herodian ashlars. The bedrock is sixty-eight feet below the plaza.

Solomon built the First Temple, which was destroyed by the Babylonians in 586 BC. The Second Temple was built on the site by Ezra and Nehemiah between 538 and 532 BC. It stood for nearly six hundred years. During his reign, Herod the Great reconstructed this temple. In 70, it was destroyed by the Romans, and the Jews exiled. The exact location of these temples is not known for certain.

DOME OF THE ROCK

The Dome of the Rock is an Islamic shrine, not a mosque, built by Umayy Abd al-Malik ibn Marwan on the site formerly occupied by the Roman temple of Jupiter and before that by the Second Temple of the Jews. An inscription in the building notes the date of completion as 691-692. It is believed to be built over the site where Abraham expressed a willingness to sacrifice Isaac and the locale from which Muhammad ascended into Heaven. The gold dome is made of gilt aluminum and bronze overlaid with eighty kilograms of gold worth over $1.4 million. It is not to be confused with the silver-domed Al-Aqsa Mosque also located on the Temple Mount.

The silver-domed Al-Aqsa Mosque stands on the area Muslims call the Noble Sanctuary, known to Jews as the Temple Mount. Its site, along with the imposing Dome of the Rock, all gates, and the plaza, was once known as the Al-Aqsa Mosque. Today only the silver-domed mosque is so designated. It is widely held that a third temple will be built on the Temple Mount.

Though access to the mount has long been available at several sites, now non-Muslims must enter through the Mughrabi Gate near the Western Wall. Israeli security controls this entry.

POOL OF SILOAM

On the lower southwest side of the Lower City of David is a manmade pool known as the Pool of Siloam. The recently excavated pool is two hundred feet long, with fifteen steps divided into three segments of five steps each with a broad landing between each segment. It is located at the end of the Siloam Tunnel, also commonly called Hezekiah's Tunnel. It is fed by water from Gihon Spring which is on the east side through Hezekiah's Tunnel that was dug in the eighth century BC. The water flows through the 1,780-foot conduit cut through solid rock that connects Gihon Spring with the Pool of Siloam. The water source being outside the city walls made the city vulnerable in the event of a siege. To protect the spring, it was covered and camouflaged to obscure it from invaders while providing a source of water for the inhabitants of the city.

The tunnel is thought to have been built during Hezekiah's time to supply the city secretly in the event of a siege by Sennacherib. A second reason for digging the tunnel is that the city grew on the southwest side, and the tunnel was needed to supply that section with water.

The tunnel was dug by two teams working from opposite ends and meeting in the middle. How this engineering marvel was accomplished is a mystery. It is postulated there was potentially a crevasse in the bedrock through which water seeped and the dig followed that fault line.

In addition to being a source of water for the city, the pool was frequented by the sick and poor who came there to bathe. The oral law of the time designated it as the Messiah's Pool. It was here Jesus sent the blind man to be healed (John 9: 6 - 9).

Water was brought from the pool to the Temple in a golden vessel on the last day of the celebration of the Feast of Tabernacles.

POOL OF BETHESDA

The Pool of Bethesda was for years a lost mystery. The site was rediscovered in 1888 during the renovation of Saint Anne's Church.

It was a spring-fed pool alleged to have five porches. Belief was the waters had healing qualities. Here Jesus healed a man who had been lame for thirty-eight years (John 5: 2 - 9).

The pool is described as having five porticoes, suggesting a five-sided pool. Excavation revealed a rectangular pool with two basins separated by a wall, thus a five-sided pool, each having a portico. The southern basin had broad steps with landings, suggesting it was a *mikver* with fresh water. The northern basin served as a reservoir, *otzer*, to continually supply fresh water which flowed through a dam between the two.

UPPER ROOM, THE COENACULUM

Jesus assembled with His disciples for their last supper together in an upper room (Luke 22: 12). Today the site commemorating that eventful gathering is on Mount Zion outside the Old City, about one hundred yards south of Zion Gate. The present facility was built in the twelfth century by Crusaders above a place designated as David's tomb. Archaeological evidence of the lower level reveals an early Roman presence. This indicates that the site of the actual Last Supper could have been in this location, the Upper Room.

Two other biblical events are associated with the site. On the day of Pentecost, Simon Peter said, "Let me speak freely to you about the patriarch David, that he is both dead and buried, and his tomb is with us yet" (Acts 2: 29). Based on this text David is represented as being entombed on the ground level of the building. The tradition naming this as the burial place of David dates back to the first or second century BC. Because it is an extra-large cenotaph (sepulcher) dating back to the Crusaders' period, it is associated with royalty. There is no way of knowing who is buried here. However, investigations in 1859 show a small empty tomb is beneath the cenotaph, indicating no one is buried there.

The exact location of the burial site of David has not been established. Archaeological efforts have not linked it with the original Old City of David. Further, efforts to place it in Bethlehem have also proven futile.

Another tradition is that the Holy Spirit descended here on the disciples after the resurrection of Jesus Christ (Acts 2: 1 - 4).

MOUNT OF OLIVES

The Mount of Olives is a north-south ridge that forms the eastern bank of the Kidron Valley or Valley of Jehoshaphat opposite Mount Zion, the Old City of Jerusalem. This limestone ridge is approximately three miles in length. In the Bible era it was densely populated with olive groves.

The crest of the mountain currently is the site of Al-Tur, a mostly Muslim village and part of East Jerusalem. The southernmost part of the Mount of Olives is known as the Mount of Scandal because Solomon built altars there to the pagan gods Ashtoreth, Chemosh, and Molech (II Kings 23: 13).

The Church of Dominus Flevit commemorates the spot on the slopes from which Jesus viewed Jerusalem and wept over the city (Matthew 26: 75). He spent time there teaching His disciples and prophesying (Matthew 24 - 25).

Alexander the Great first viewed the city from a prominent spot on the northern end of the Mount of Olives which he named Mount Scopus, Lookout Hill.

The Roman general Titus and his 10th Legion camped on the north end during their siege of Jerusalem. After the destruction of the Second Temple in 70, the mountain became the destination of Jews who came to view the Temple Mount. Since Mount Scopus is two hundred and sixty-four feet higher than the Temple Mount, it provides a panoramic view of the Temple location. Presently on the ninth day of the Hebrew month of Av, the anniversary of the destruction of the Temple, a time of lamentation for the destruction is still observed.

The first mention of the mount in Scripture described David's going there during his conflict with his son Absalom (II Samuel 15:30).

The Chapel of Ascension marks a spot where Jesus is said to

have ascended into heaven. The slopes of the mountain have been a cemetery for over three thousand years, and more than a hundred and fifty thousand persons are buried there. The traditional Tombs of the Prophets Haggai, Zechariah, and Malachi are among them.

Prominent on the side of the mountain is the Church of St. Mary of Magdala with its seven golden, onion-shaped domes, each capped with a cross, a prominent feature on the mount.

At the foot of the mountain where it meets the Kidron Valley is the Garden of Gethsemane. The olive trees here are believed to have grown from the root system of trees from the time of Jesus. Olive trees do not have growth rings like most trees; therefore, it is impossible to date them exactly. In the garden is the Church of All Nations which houses an outcropping of rock where it is said Jesus prayed before His arrest (Matthew 14: 32ff). The current church rests on the foundation of two former churches on the site dating back to the twelfth century. One of the former churches dated from the Byzantine period and the other from the Crusaders' period. The present church was consecrated in June 1924.

One of the three paths from the valley to the summit is known as the Psalm Sunday Road, leading from Jerusalem to Bethany. It is held that down this road Jesus proceeded on His last visit to Jerusalem.

Prophetically, Zechariah refers to the Mount of Olives playing a strategic role in the future Day of the Lord: "In that day His feet will stand on the Mount of Olives, which faces Jerusalem on the east. And the Mount of Olives shall be split in two from the east to west, making a very large valley; half of the mountain shall move toward the north and half of it toward the south" (Zechariah 14: 4).

THE CRUCIFIXION OF JESUS

Who killed Jesus Christ?

Individuals, not a race of people, did it. The disciples who supported Jesus were Jews. The Scripture makes it clear that the common people, the Jewish populace, responded warmly to Him. He was buried by compassionate Jews. It is true that some Jews were in part responsible for His death; however, Jews were not leaders of the crucifixion.

Romans (Gentiles or non-Jews) in the persons of Pilate and his execution squad were involved in the physical act. They carried out the execution. It was Gentiles who pinioned Him to the cross.

Jesus was brought before the seventy-one-member Sanhedrin, the Jewish Supreme Court, at night. Twenty-three was considered a quorum. Here charges were formulated against Him. The first charge was that He had said He would restore the Temple in three days if it were destroyed. His statement was figurative language referring to His death and resurrection. This was twisted to mean He Himself would destroy the Temple. To this charge Jesus did not respond. The law did not compel Him to answer.

The timing not being right, Jesus had repeatedly warned His disciples not to tell anyone He was the Messiah. Evidently in his betrayal of Christ, Judas told the authorities. The High Priest asked the ultimate question, "Are you the Messiah?"

"No," would have ended the trial. His "yes" sealed His death warrant.

When morning came, the chief priest and elders took Jesus to the Roman governor, Pilate. They knew that only the Roman governor could pronounce a sentence of death. They also knew Pilate could not care less about their religious charges. They brought three new false charges: He was a revolutionary, He incited the people not to pay taxes, and He claimed to be a king. As procurator, Pilate was answerable to Caesar. Pilate, a Gentile, vacillated, tried to shift the blame, and eventually declared himself innocent of the blood of Jesus. Finally, he pronounced the death sentence. His death squad carried out the sentence of crucifixion.

The charges were brought by some religious leaders who were Jews. The actual act of execution was performed by some Romans who were Gentiles. There were both Jews and Romans who supported Him. In fact, at the cross the Roman centurion who was the chief executor said, "Surely, this was the Son of God."

Not all of the Jews or Romans killed Jesus. It was some Jews and some Romans who partnered in His execution.

Jewish law of the era stated, "In the trial of life, if thou sinnest, the blood of the accused and the blood of his seed unto the end of time shall be imputed unto thee." Even this does not apply to an entire race, but rather to those persons who were involved.

If it was as Scripture teaches that He died for "all mankind," then each person is as responsible as the persons who brought the charges and those who drove the spikes. The responsible race is the human race. For responsive members of that race He prayed, "Father, forgive them for they know not what they do."

From about the sixth century BC to the fourth century BC, crucifixion was a common form of execution practiced by the Romans. It was considered so heinous that Roman citizens were forbidden to look at it. Constantine, the first Christian emperor, abolished it in the early fourth century out of veneration for Jesus Christ.

It was so common that there was no conventional way in which every person was crucified. The substance and shape of the cross often varied. The placement of the nails in either the hands or wrists varied. The executioners had no class or style.

The reed used to offer Jesus liquid on the cross grew to a length of about eighteen inches. This would indicate His head would have been approximately nine feet off the ground.

At the time Jesus was crucified, a wedge was placed in such a location as to afford some support of the body. Wedges for the feet began to be used later.

There are those who insist Jesus did not die on the cross, but only swooned. They need to take into consideration conditions that modern science reveals what would happen to anyone being crucified.

Blood and fluid loss would have produced hypovolemia, causing the blood pressure to drop; hypertension, causing the heart rate to increase; and tachycardia, leading to cardiovascular collapse.

The position of the subject's arms would result in a loss of strength, contributing to suffocation. The lack of air in the lungs would result in low oxygen, hypoxemia, and high carbon dioxide, hypercapnia. These combined conditions, along with others, would cause cardia arrhythmia, abnormal heart beat, and fibrillation of the heart muscle that could not sustain life.

In effect, Christ died two deaths on the cross: one spiritually and one physically.

In speaking of His dying spiritually, it is not meant He ceased to exist spiritually. Spiritual death was the reference when God told Adam that if he ate of the tree he would die (Genesis 3:17). Adam remained physically alive for some time after eating. However, in the moment of disobedience, he died spiritually; that is, he was separated from God.

About midday when Christ cried from the cross, "My God, my God, why have you forsaken me?" (Matthew 27: 46), He was separated from the Father. That is, He died spiritually though He was still alive physically.

About 3:00 PM Christ cried, "It is finished" (John 19:30). His role in providing for the forgiveness of sin was complete.

When He said, "Father, into your hands I commend my spirit," He was saying, "Spirit, you are now released to go be with the Father." That was the moment He died physically (Luke 23: 46). In that instant, spiritually He was reunited with His partners in the Trinity.

We tend to get so absorbed in the horror of Christ's physical death that we overlook the significance of His spiritual death. Again, it should be noted, spiritual death is separation from God. That was the horror of His crucifixion, not only the physical anguish. That is the condition of every lost person in the state of sin.

"He made Him who knew no sin to be sin for us, that we might become the righteousness of God in Him" (II Corinthians 5:21). When Christ took upon Himself the sin of the world, He was in the state of every lost person, spiritually dead and separated from the Father.

The ultimate conclusion is this: Since God is infinite, we cannot possibly understand all that transpired in that dismal period on the cross.

JESUS' RESURRECTION, THE TOMB GUARDS

Immediately after the crucifixion, the chief priest and Pharisees visited Pilate and reminded him of Jesus' words "After three days I will rise." To prevent the disciples from stealing the body and claiming a resurrection, they asked Pilate for a guard to be posted at the tomb. Pilate replied, "You have a guard..." (Matthew 27: 63, 64).

Jerusalem at the time was overcrowded because it was the Day of Preparation. Every soldier available was needed to help keep order in the city. Pilate knew that because of a recent conflict there were no soldiers to spare.

Phasaelis, the daughter of Aretas IV, king of the Nabataeans, had married Herod, the Tetrarch. When Phasaelis learned Herod planned to divorce her and marry Herodias, the wife of his brother Herod Philip, she fled to her father, Aretas IV. He was angered by the treatment given his daughter. He marched his army up the east bank of the Dead Sea, encountered Herod's army, and decimated them. Had not Rome intervened, he would have completely overthrown Herod's army. As it was, Herod had left his army so undermanned that there were not enough soldiers to allow some to serve at the tomb.

People reading the statement "You have a guard" assume Pilate is saying, "I am giving you a guard." What he meant by the statement was, "You have your own Temple Guard. Use them to guard the tomb."

The guards at the tomb were not Roman soldiers, but Jews who were members of the Temple Guard. That is all the more important because they of all people would want to ensure the safekeeping of the corpse.

THREE DAYS AND THREE NIGHTS

Of His impending death and resurrection Jesus said, "For as Jonah was three days and three nights in the belly of the great fish, so will the Son of Man be three days and three nights in the heart of the earth" (Mathew 12: 40).

If crucified on Friday and found to be resurrected on Sunday morning, how is that counted as three days and nights? The challenge is resolved in how time is counted today and how it was counted in the Bible era:

- Today a day is considered as starting at daylight with night following the daylight. In the Jewish tradition a day began at sundown and ended at the following sundown.
- Today a day is considered as a full twenty-four hours. In the Jewish tradition any part of a day was considered as a full day. Hence, a day was not necessarily twenty hours.
- When the sun set on Thursday, that was considered the night part of Friday. Therefore, Friday was one day and one night.
- Friday night at sundown, day two began.
- Saturday at sundown, day three began. Sunrise on Sunday was the day part of day three. In the Jewish tradition of considering time, this was three days and three nights.

SAINT PETER IN CALLICANTU

The impressive Church of St. Peter in Gallicantu is located on the eastern slope of Mount Zion. Gallicantu in Latin means cockcrow. It exemplifies Peter's three-time denial of Jesus after His arrest. Atop the church is a large black cross with a golden rooster on top. All four gospels make reference to the denial, with Matthew being the most distinct (Matthew 26: 69 - 75).

The Assumptionist Church is built over the ruins of a Byzantine basilica thought to be the place of Peter's denial.

It consists of four levels: upper church, middle church, guardroom, and dungeon. In the courtyard is a statue depicting a rooster, the woman questioning Peter, and a Roman soldier.

The lower level is believed to be the guardroom and place of the imprisonment of Jesus on the night of His betrayal. The prisoner would have been lowered into the cell through a shaft by rope. It would have been a foreboding, solitary place.

Affixed to the walls are fixtures to which prisoners could have been chained. Holes in the columns could have been used to tie prisoners while they were flogged. Bowls carved in the floor would have contained vinegar and salt into which whips could be dipped, thus intensifying the pain.

Outside the church are steep steps leading from Mount Zion to the Kedron Valley. It is highly probable Jesus would have descended these steps on his last night as He made His way to Gethsemane.

HEROD'S PALACE

Herod's palace and the praetorium have, in recent years, been determined to be in the area of the Tower of David. The discovery takes on extra meaning in that it would have been the place where Herod received the "wise men from the east" who came seeking the new-born "King of the Jews" (Matthew 1: 2).

Of equal importance is that it would have been where Jesus was put on trial before Pilate.

The location near the Tower of David has long been studied as the possible site of Herod's palace. Since the 1960s, archaeological teams have uncovered various parts of the substructure, but almost none of the superstructure. It was confirmed as the site of the palace in 2001, but that revelation has only recently been called to the attention of the public because the site was not in a condition to be opened to the public prior to 2017.

A confluence of archaeology and biblical references indicates the trial may have been at the newly excavated site of Herod's palace. If accepted, this would make a seismic shift in the proposed site of the trial and the route to Calvary.

Recent discoveries suggest a different scenario regarding Jesus' having been on trial before Pilate at the Fortress Antonio and the route to Calvary being the long-held tradition of the Via Dolorosa. The fortress and route are themselves traditions. In the mid-fourth century, Constantine was the first to have a route proposed. The current one was established in the eighteenth century, replacing previously suggested routes. Various modifications as to where what happened have been made since then.

Historian Josephus reported that the palace was begun during the last quarter of the first century BC. The palace was not a single building, but a compound containing a palatial residence, guest quarters, gardens, pools, fountains, and military barracks. Josephus further noted, "It was enormous, with a lot of gold and silver and running water, and guest quarters." It was protected by three large towers on the northwest corner of the precinct.

In Jerusalem during the biblical era, the palace was second only to the Temple in importance.

From medieval times, tradition has located the praetorium near the Fortress Antonia in the northeast part of the Old City. It has now been concluded that the Antonia would have been too small to have been the residence and headquarters of the governor. The fortress was basically a military compound with its purpose being to serve as an observation tower overlooking the Temple Mount. Today the praetorium is associated with Herod's palace on the western side of the city.

After Herod's death, the palace became the official residence of the Roman governors when they visited Jerusalem. The Roman custom was for a new official who replaced the previous authority to symbolize a transfer of power by living in the residence of the previous authority. As such, it would have been the residence of

Pontius Pilate at the time of the trial of Jesus.

This being true, the traditional Via Dolorosa used by tourists to commemorate the steps of Jesus on His way to the cross would be controverted. Authorities at the Tower of David Museum are hopeful that pilgrims will eventually accept the authenticity of the new point of origin, and they are proposing a new route to the Church of the Holy Sepulcher.

The exact location of these holy places may never be proven. In walking a proposed route, pilgrims should commemorate the event, not sanctify the site. To change a tradition is always challenging. A paradigm shift such as this is made more difficult in that more than a million pilgrims walk the Via Dolorosa each year.

ANNAS' PALATIAL MANSION

Excavated in recent years, within the Old City are the remains of a luxurious residence. In recent time, it has been suggested as a potential replacement for Saint Peter in Gallicantu as the place of Jesus' first trial. There are some qualifying features: a high priestly house, a view of the courtyard from inside the house, and, most of all, its proximity to the Temple Mount. This location would make the High Priest accessible for Temple service. Also, from here priests could cross to the Temple Mount by way of the Royal Bridge and not have to go through the Tyropoeon Valley.

Destroyed by the Roman siege in 70, the opulence of the ruins is impressive. It was restored in 1985—1987. It was surely a residence of a very important person. The square footage of each of two floors was   sixty-five hundred feet. No other such house has ever been found in Israel.

It was not likely the house of either Pilate or Herod because their residences were elsewhere. Only Caiaphas would have been of enough fame and wealth to afford such a palatial place. Having controlled the Temple finances which Jesus described as "a house of thieves," Caiaphas was a wealthy man. Technically, Annas' son-in-law

Caiaphas was High Priest, but Annas, having been High Priest from 6 to 15, still bore the title of High Priest and had residual power. He was, after all, the *éminence grise* who exercised power by promoting members of his own family to priestly roles. John 18:13 mentions Jesus being taken to the High Priest first.

In the house, one comes into the vestibule. To the right is a magnificent reception room. Straight forward from the vestibule is the courtyard around which the house was built. From the center of the reception room where the hearing would have been held, two doorways lead into the courtyard. This is how Jesus could have seen Peter in the courtyard around the fire.

Traces of a great deal of flagellation have been found in the Palace Mansion, providing further validation for the area.

As with so many events noted in the Bible, optional places are offered today as to where the actual event transpired. This one is worthy of consideration as the place where Jesus appeared before Annas.

THE STATIONS OF THE CROSS

The Via Dolorosa, variously called Way of the Cross, Way of Sorrow, Way of Grief, and Suffering Way, is a street in the Old City of Jerusalem reputed to be the street Jesus walked on His way to the cross. This tradition was begun in the medieval period. It is highly unlikely to be the actual route but is a special place to commemorate His historical walk. The fourteen Stations of the Cross along the route are not actual places where the acts represented occurred. Six of the fourteen are based on tradition, not actual happenings.

Every Friday at 3:00 PM, there is a procession of pilgrims along the route. It is thought the concept of establishing Stations of the Cross was begun in Europe by Christians who could not go to the Bible Land but still wanted to reflect on Jesus' agony. Over the years, the number of stations has varied from seven to eighteen. The practice on the Via Dolorosa was begun in the eighteenth century. Eight of the stations are based on Bible texts. The other six represent three alleged falls by Jesus, His meeting with His mother, and Veronica wiping His face—again, which are tradition only. The last five are within the Church of the Holy Sepulcher, including the last traditional one, Jesus' body laid in the Sepulcher.

The *Ecce Homo Arch*, meaning Behold the Man, spans the Via Dolorosa near the beginning of the route. It represents the place where Pilate presented Jesus to the crowd saying, "Behold the man."

The stations are these:

1.   Jesus is condemned (Matthew 27: 26 - 31).

2.   Jesus takes up His cross (John 19: 17).

3.   Jesus falls the first time (Lore).

4.   Jesus meets Mary (Lore).

5.   Simon of Cyrene helps carry the cross (Mark 15: 21).

6.   Veronica wipes the face of Jesus (Lore).

7.   Jesus falls the second time (Lore).

8.   Jesus consoles the women of Jerusalem (Luke 23: 27 - 31).

9.   Jesus falls the third time (Lore).

The following are in the Church of the Holy Sepulcher:

10.   Jesus is stripped of His garments (John 19: 23).

11.   Jesus is nailed to the cross (Luke 23: 33).

12.   Jesus dies on the cross (Mark 15: 31).

13.   Jesus' body is embraced by Mary (Lore).

14.   Jesus is laid in the tomb (Matthew 27: 59, 60).

The exact location of each station is not of the greatest importance. The walk has great meaning because of the proximity to the actual events.

THE LAND

MEGIDDO

Movement through the heartland of the Galilee required passage through Megiddo.

The city of Megiddo dates back roughly eight thousand years. The city ceased to exist after the Persian invasion of Palestine some twenty-three hundred years ago, and today nothing is left but the ruins of what once was a regional administrative and military center during the reign of King Solomon.

Archaeologists working in Megiddo have unearthed an incredible twenty-five layers of settlement built on top of each other covering a period of thirty-five centuries. It was the setting of numerous battles. He who controlled Megiddo controlled the Jezreel Valley, the Sea Highway, and most of the commerce of the entire region.

Megiddo's long history is related to its strategic position overlooking the Via Maris, one of the main routes used for travel between Egypt, Syria, and Mesopotamia. The city is referred to in the New Testament as Armageddon, a name John derived from the Hebrew for Mount Megiddo, *Harad Megiddo*. According to the book of Revelation, this is where the last great battle will be fought when the forces of good will triumph over evil.

Pharaoh Thutmose III claimed in the fifteenth century BC, "Capturing Megiddo is as good as capturing one thousand cities."

When King Thutmose III of Egypt did conquer Megiddo thirty-five hundred years ago, among other things he left with were 1,929 head of cattle, 2,000 goats, 20,500 sheep, 204 horses, 200 army uniforms, and 502 bows.

The first people to inhabit Megiddo arrived during the Neolithic period. A watershed period occurred in the twentieth century BC when it became a fortified city-state. Egypt later dominated the area then known as Canaan, and massive walls were built around the city, which indicate Megiddo had become wealthy and required protection.

The first written reference to Megiddo—indeed the first recorded battle in history—is a detailed account of the 1479 BC invasion by the Egyptian Pharaoh Thutmose III. The city subsequently became a center of culture and politics.

The waters of Megiddo (Judges 5: 19) had their source outside the city walls. To secretly access it, a tunnel was built from Ahab's shaft in the city to the spring. The shaft is one hundred twenty feet deep and the tunnel two hundred fifteen feet to the spring. A narrow stone spiraling stair in the shaft was used by persons hauling water. The tunnel at one point was hewn so that the water from the spring outside the walls flowed to the base of the shaft. This allowed inhabitants to draw the water as though it were a well.

To conceal the source of the city's water outside the walls and hide it from invaders, a camouflaged wall was built to obscure it.

VALLEY OF ARMAGEDDON

The Jezreel Valley, referred to as the Valley of Armageddon, has a triangular shape of about twelve miles on each side. It is the junction point of several major north-south trade and military routes, including the Via Maris (the Way of the Sea) highway which linked Egypt in the south with Anatolia in the north. The name is associated with Judgment Day, apocalypse, and end times. It generates visions of a cataclysmic end-time battle between the forces of evil and good.

The name appears only once in the New Testament, Revelation 16: 16. The Bible does not specifically mention armies gathering in the valley, but rather that "they (will gather) the kings together to ...Armageddon." The text strongly suggests the purpose of the gathering will be "for the war of the great day of God, the Almighty" (Revelation 16: 14).

The valley is credited with having seen more bloodshed than any place on earth. Innumerable battles have been fought on these fields. An area fought over by two forces, neither of which are from the area, is called contested periphery. Almost one third of the battles fought here have been contested periphery.

The index of armies that have fought in the valley is lengthy: Egyptian, Israelite, Greek, Muslim, Crusader, Mongol, British, and Arab. The outcome of many of the battles changed nations.

The first battle recorded to have been fought here pitted the Egyptian forces under Pharaoh Thutmose III against a large rebellious coalition of Canaanite states. Records of the date vary, but it was circa 1480 BC. It is the first battle in history to report a body count.

Two great victories influencing Israel have been fought on this plain. One on the eastern side involved Deborah and Barak defeating the Canaanites (Judges 3, 4). The second was Gideon's victory over the Midianites (Judges 7).

Two great defeats and deaths influencing Israel also occurred here. One on the eastern side near Beit She'an involved King Saul and his sons who were killed (I Samuel 31: 8). The other was the death of King Josiah (II Kings 23: 29, 30 & II Chronicles 35: 22). The Philistines killed Saul's sons, and Saul fell on his own sword at Mount Gilboa (I Samuel 31: 4). His self-inflicted wound was not fatal. Saul pleaded with a young opposing warrior to deliver a fatal blow after asking who he was. His answer has in it irony: "I am an Amalekite" (II Samuel 1: 8). He was one whose life was spared in Saul's disobedience to God (I Samuel 15: 18, 19).

One epic battle that changed the course of history involved British General Allenby, who won the battle over the Turks in 1918, causing them to relinquish control of the region of Palestine to the British. This ended the control of the area by the Ottoman Empire and began the British control which lasted until 1948. In 1947 the United Nations partitioned the region and mandated a portion be given to the Jews and part to the Arabs. The current conditions of the region have evolved from this decision.

There are numerous schools of thought regarding the final battle. One primary one holds it is to be fought in the Jezreel Valley on the field of Armageddon. It will be a pinnacle conflict between the Antichrist and the Messiah. The kings, world leaders, will have conspired and gathered their forces against Israel. Scripture notes that is their purpose. In keeping with this concept, the following is thought to relate as God's counter purpose: "My determination is to gather the nations to My assembly of kingdoms, to pour on them My indignation..." (Zephaniah 3: 8).

One counter school of thought holds that the Battle of Armageddon is a figurative summary of an end-time confrontation bespeaking of God's ultimate victory over evil.

Christians are reminded that they are to be ever aware that "The secret things belong to our God..." (Deuteronomy 29: 29).

MOUNT TABOR

Eleven miles west of the Sea of Galilee at the eastern end of the Jezreel Valley, the dome-shaped Mount Tabor rises 1,886 feet above the plain and is crowned by the Church of the Transfiguration. It was built between 1919 and 1924 on the ruins of a Byzantine church to commemorate Jesus' transfiguration (Matthew 17: 2). It is highly unlikely to have been the location. Scripture notes that Jesus "brought them up on a high mountain by themselves" (Matthew 17: 1). A military fort was located on top of the mountain at the time, preventing it being a place of solitude.

Nearby is a small cave-church named for Melchizedek, King of Salem. Tradition holds it is the place where Abraham was greeted by Melchizedek.

Its imposing image is first used in the Bible as an illustration of majesty: "Surely one will come who looms up like Tabor among the mountains..." (Psalm 89: 12).

Of the many battles fought on or near it, the conflict between the Israelite tribes under the leadership of Deborah, God's appointed judge over Israel, and her field general Barak against the overpowering Canaanite army of Sisera, which consisted of nine hundred chariots of iron (Judges 4: 3) is meaningful. At a strategic time in the battle, a rainstorm blowing in the faces of the Canaanite force and flooding the battlefield resulted in the chariots bogging down and the Canaanites being defeated. Scripture indicates that the Canaanites were swept away by the swollen waters of the Kishon River" (Judges 5: 19 - 210).

Another battle fought at or on Mount Tabor was highly significant. The Mongol leader Hulaguh defeated powerful armies across Asia and Europe, and his army of a hundred thousand were advancing toward Jerusalem when confronted by the Mameluke army of Sultan Qutuz near the base of Mount Tabor. Most of the Mamelukes were Kipchaks, and their Golden Hoard replenished the Mamelukes, enabling their victory. This turned back the Mongol occupation of the land.

The area changed hands several times during the Crusades and became a Christian tourist destination.

SEPPHORIS

Sepphoris is an ancient Greek city in lower Galilee, a short distance from Nazareth. The ingenuity and artistic skills of the people are evident based on modern archaeology which has unearthed several magnificent mosaics. A richly colored mosaic portrait of an unnamed woman was discovered among the ruins. The enchanting tilt of her head and near-smile earned her the nickname Mona Lisa of the Galilee. Using tiny stones in a wide range of natural colors, the artist depicts subtle variances between her features, including her bright earrings, the shades of her clothes, the gloss of her lips, and the flush of her cheeks.

The people of Sepphoris had exceptional engineering skill, enabling them to creatively design an aqueduct that ran from a distant mountain around the edge of another and ended in an enormous reservoir in the city. The beauty of the city earned it the title of The Ornament of All Galilee, given it by historian Josephus.

Around 4 BC, the Roman army headed by Varus quelled a rebellion in Sepphoris and burned the city. The reconstruction undertaken by Herod Antipas was still in progress in the time of Jesus. There being little work in Nazareth, Joseph would logically have made the four-mile trip to Sepphoris to work.

It is traditionally considered the hometown of Anne and Joachim, the parents of Mary and grandparents of Jesus, making it logical that young Jesus would have visited there often. Much of His formal education may well have been achieved in one of the city's many synagogues. Being located on major trade routes made it a prime market. This would have given the young Jesus an opportunity to become familiar with urban life and other cultures.

Sepphoris is not credited biblically as playing a part in the obscure early years of Jesus. The ethos of Nazareth would not have prepared Jesus for the larger stage awaiting him. That of Sepphoris would have.

ACRE

Awash in the spray from the Haifa Bay is the city of Acre, which linked the inland commercial routes with the sea. It is one of the oldest continually inhabited cities in the world. Early reference was made to it in the time of Pharaoh Thutmose III (1504 - 1450 BC). Acre has existed for at least forty-five hundred years but reached its zenith under Crusader rule. Alleys, streets, and tunnels make for a labyrinthine community. As a seaport, it once was as viable as Alexandria and Constantinople. Among the conquerors of the city are Crusaders, Muslims, and Ottomans. Napoleon failed in his attempt to conquer the city.

Upon conquering it, the Crusaders named it for St. Jean d'Acre, thus Acre.

Spelled *Akko,* it means the gift of God. In 1219, the Mamelukes destroyed the city and killed all the remaining Crusaders. This reduced the city to a minor role for over five hundred years. The existing city was built by the Ottoman Turks around 1750. Since that time, many of the older sections have been preserved.

The subterranean Crusader city enables one to walk down to different levels of the underground city. Captivating is the Hospitaller Knights' Hall used as a fortress more than seven hundred years ago. The lowest level is the Crypt, a great hall. The Templar's Tunnel with its gothic vaulted hall runs from the city to the seaport. It was used by the Knights as an evacuation passage when the city was overrun by the Turks.

Acre (Akko) is mentioned in the Old Testament in Judges 1:31 and in the New Testament under the name Ptolemais (Acts 21:7).

It is an ever-increasing modern tourist destination.

GALILEE

The area around the Sea of Galilee is so captivating and home to so much of Jesus' ministry; even the sardonic Mark Twain wrote of it in *The Innocents Abroad*.

In the starlight, Galilee has no boundaries but the broad compass of the heavens, and is a theater meet for great events; meet for the birth of a religion able to save a world; and meet for the stately Figure appointed to stand upon its stage and proclaim its high decrees. But in the sunlight, one says: Is it for the deeds which were done and the words which were spoken in this little acre of rocks and sand eighteen centuries gone, that the bells are ringing to-day in the remote islands of the sea and far and wide over continents that clasp the circumference of the huge globe?

The region of Galilee became the ideal site for Jesus to live and minister. The vicinity around the lower Jordan Valley was not suitable because the people had been incited by the arrest of John the Baptist there.

Jerusalem was not an option as a result of the bitter resentment of the biased religious leaders. In His hometown of Nazareth, He was an object of derision as a result of His claiming to be the fulfillment of Scripture regarding Messiah.

The process of elimination, if nothing else, resulted in cities such as Capernaum, Korezin, Bethsaida, and Magdala along the shores of the Sea of Galilee becoming His home. The Sea is located in northeast Israel between the Golan Heights and the region Galilee. Historically, the area has been impacted by earthquakes and volcanic activity which have deposited large quantities of basil and igneous rock in the region.

Though being the size of a large lake, it is called a sea because there was no Hebrew word for sea. Only the gospel of Luke uses a word for it calling it the Lake of Gennesaret (Luke 5: 1). The Sea is the lowest large freshwater lake on earth. Only the saltwater Dead Sea is lower. Its lowest depth is about a hundred and forty feet. It is fed principally by the Mount Hermon watershed which flows into the Sea through the Jordan River. Fresh water springs are also a source of supply. Shaped like a harp, it is also known as Kinneret, from the Hebrew word for harp, *kinor*.

It has served in recent years as the primary source of water for irrigation and human use in Israel. Recent dramatic progress in distillation has resulted in the need for a supply of fresh water in the country being greatly reduced.

Skeptics have questioned why Jesus did not go to major metropolitan cities such as Athens or Rome.

The *Via Mora*, the Sea Highway, trade route connecting Europe, Asia, and Africa turned inland as it neared here in order to gain access to the fresh water of the Sea of Galilee. The routes from Arabia came up the Jordan Valley, and tradesmen on these routes would have heard Him teach.

Hot springs at Hammat Tiberias, known as healing spas, were at the southwest corner of the sea. They attracted people from three continents.

Instead of Jesus going to distant people, they came to Him. Among those masses that heard Him teach and observed His miracles were people from a vast region. The crowds did not consist of local peasants only. Among the masses to pass through the region would have been scholars, wealthy merchants, and public figures.

This was the Grand Central Station in the Middle East at the time.

Near the end of His ministry, Greeks came wanting to see Jesus. Doubtless, members of caravans who had heard Him in Galilee had carried news of His ministry home. Before Paul and others began to spread the message of Jesus abroad, He and His teaching were known far beyond the Galilee.

The topography of an area along the coast known as The Sowers Cove or the Bay of the Parables forms somewhat of a natural amphitheater where large crowds could easily hear a speaker. Acoustical tests have proven as many as seven thousand people could hear a speaker here. It was an ideal setting for Jesus to teach large crowds.

Even nature gave illustrative support to Jesus' teaching. This section of Galilee is in the Jordan Rift Valley. The warm air coming up the valley invites the cooler air coming from the upland around Mount Arbel and through the Arbel Valley, causing sudden and violent storms on the sea. One such storm frightened the apostles who were on the sea and Jesus was asleep in the boat. Being awakened, He calmed the sea.

MOUNT ARBEL

Mount Arbel rises thirteen hundred feet above the Plain of Gennesaret like a sentinel over the Galilee. Running parallel with the ridge is the Valley of the Doves. The two merge to form a wind tunnel producing unexpected high winds on the Sea of Galilee.

The valley is a trade route and ideal roadway from Nazareth to Capernaum. It would have been a logical route for Jesus to travel between the two cities.

The mountain has seen so much bloodshed it is referred to as

Bloody Arbel. The Assyrians slaughtered a great number of Jews by forcing them off heights of the cliffs.

In 161 BC, the Seleucid General Bacchides captured the mountain after a great slaughter.

Another momentous battle that occurred in 39 BC was described by Josephus Flavius as the "battle of the cave men against the cage men." The face of the mountain is a honeycomb of caves, many of which have multiple rooms. Zealots were entrenched in the caves. Soldiers of Herod the Great were lowered in cages to the mouths of the caves on the sheer north side and dragged people out with hooks throwing them over the ramparts.

After the destruction of the Temple in Jerusalem, the Yeshua course of priests settled on the crest.

There is no mention of the mountain in the New Testament. However, it is speculated it was the high mountain the resurrected Jesus took His disciples to share the Great Commission related to global evangelism. Jesus is noted as having visited the towns in Galilee, leading to speculation He visited the cities on the mountain (Matthew 9: 35). Because of the long shadow it casts, some believe it to be the reference related to the "land of the shadow of death" (Isaiah 9:2).

Nearby is Nebi Shueb, a volcanic mountain known as Karnei Hattin, the Horns of Hattin. Unexplainably, on July 4, 1187, the Crusader force left their defensible positions and marched into the plain between the two mountains. Dressed in their heavy armament, being away from their water supply, dehydrated and sweltering in their heavy metal uniforms, they were vulnerable preys to Saladin's Muslim force. With the wind blowing in the faces of the Crusaders, Saladin set the field afire. Choked by the smoke the Crusaders were easy subjects for their slaughter. This battle ended the Crusader rule in the Bible Land.

Today there are four small villages at the ancient site, and in the Talmidic village of Arbel are the ruins of an ancient synagogue on the mountain. Arbel affords one of the most stunning panoramas of the Galilee.

MAGDALA

Located on the shores of the sea, Caesarea and Magdala were centers of commerce. The fishing industry was an important business attracting far distant markets. Josephus notes around that time there were forty thousand inhabitants in Magdala with the fishing fleet numbering two hundred and thirty boats.

The sea itself is only fourteen miles long and seven miles wide, but still it offers an abundance of fish. Magdala was a major first-century port on the Sea of Galilee, a center of trade and commerce throughout Europe. Jesus is said to have gone there by boat (Matthew 15: 29). Galilee was not as unknown as most assume.

In recent years, the area has been excavated, exposing the remains of an ancient synagogue dating from the first century. Jesus was said to have gone through all the cities of the area preaching in their synagogues; therefore, it is highly likely He spoke here (Matthew 9: 25).

Magdala can't be mentioned without noting it as the hometown of the iconic Mary Magdalene. It is not known if she lived there or was simply born there. She was freed from possession by seven demons. There is no Bible reference to her being a prostitute. That image emerged three hundred years later. Had she been, it is likely it would be noted in Scripture. She was obviously wealthy and became one of the women who supported Jesus from their own wealth (Luke 8: 2, 3).

Mary Magdalene is one of the few women noted in the Bible as being present at Jesus' crucifixion. She was also noted as the one to whom the resurrected Jesus appeared. Such renown prompted the Russian Orthodox Church to erect the beautiful Church of Saint Mary Magdalene on the Mount of Olives, just above the Garden of Gethsemane.

CAPERNAUM

Further up the north coast of the Sea of Galilee is Capernaum, a city that in the time of Jesus had fifteen hundred residents. It, too, was a fishing center, less than ten miles from Magdala, and served as a base of operation for Jesus. From here He called His disciples, performed miracles, healed, taught, and ventured into other areas.

Initially, the people were impressed because He taught as one with authority (Mark 1: 21, 22). Ultimately, their unbelief resulted in His putting a curse on it as well as Chorazin and Bethsaida.

In 1838, it was still desolate, deserving the description given by archaeologists who discovered it: "The whole place is desolate and mournful...."

Of significance, it was here Jesus called His first disciples. Never has a more diverse group of people bonded and then disbursed on a common mission.

There was Peter, the alpha-apostle; James the Lesser, who was no less important; Simon the Zealot; and Matthew, the quisling; John, the devotee; Judas, the betrayer; Thomas, the enquirer; and Andrew, the informer; Nathaniel, a man of royal descent; James son of Zebedee, the assertive; Philip, the provider; and James, the diligent.

Their distinct personalities often clashed and then coalesced. Matthew, a contemptuous tax collector, was on the east bank of the sea, and Peter, a fisherman, and a businessman on the west bank. Traditionally both disciples would have had instinctive disregard for each other. Matthew's district was changed to include Capernaum; and, hence, he became Peter's tax collector. Before being called by Jesus, it is logical there was angst between them.

Among those called was a man of violence, Simon the Zealot. The Zealots were a band of cutthroats who worked civilly during the day and attacked Romans by night. James and John were called Boanerges, or the Sons of Thunder, which speaks of their old nature. Peter proved to have an impetuous nature. All were flawed, but only one was a failure, Judas.

Jesus spent time with them, tempering them as a smith would fine steel.

Beneath an octagonal church in Capernaum is a first-century home reputed to be Peter's. Scripture notes Jesus "entered Peter's house and saw his mother-in-law lying sick with a fever..." (Matthew 8: 14). Later that same evening, He was still at Peter's house (Matthew 8: 16). After being away, "He entered Capernaum after some days, and it was heard He was in the house" (Mark 2: 1).

A Catholic Church with a glass floor built over Peter's house enables visitors to peer into the ruins. Since the first century, one room has been identified as distinct. Graffiti on a plastered wall written in Greek references Jesus as "Lord and Christ." If this became a church, it would be the first known house church.

Graffiti left by pilgrims indicate the site has long been venerated as a special place of spiritual significance. Among the writings are "Lord Jesus Christ help thy servant..." and "Christ have mercy...."

The house consists of a cluster of rooms built around two courtyards, as was the custom from the Roman period. The location, the graffiti, and the octagonal shape of the first church built on the site indicate it to be a significant spiritual site leading to the conclusion it was a home of significance, the home of Peter. Octagonal churches were built to designate sites of special historical Christian happenings.

The synagogue in Capernaum is dated from the fourth or fifth century. The date is determined by a cache of ten thousand coins found under the synagogue floor.

That which makes the synagogue special is that if a synagogue of the era should be replaced, it was not relocated, but built on the site of the former one. The foundation of the synagogue in which Jesus would have taught has been excavated. On the foundation was reconstructed another synagogue in the fourth and fifth centuries.

Part of it still stands.

TIBERIAS

On the west bank of the Sea near the southern end is the modern city of Tiberias, established around 20 by Herod Antipas and named for the second Emperor of the Roman Empire. He built it from revenue gained from people who came there for healing. It was located near the several natural mineral hot springs in Hammat Tiberias.

Along with Jerusalem, Hebron, and Safed, it is considered one of Judaism's Four Holiest Cities. It is mentioned in John 6:23 as the place boats sailed to on the eastern shore of the sea. After the miraculous feeding of the five thousand, the crowds used these boats to travel back to Capernaum.

Orthodox Jews resisting Hellenization refused to settle there because of a nearby cemetery which made the area ritually unclean. Antipas moved a number of non-Jews there from throughout the region. The city grew so dramatically the sea became known as the Sea of Tiberias.

Antipas had his Roman soldiers deliberately mingle among the citizens, incurring their anger. He insisted on the people paying a certain tax regardless of whether they had a good or bad year. If the tax wasn't paid, the person lost his property, further inflaming the population.

Local Judeans were more able to pay their taxes than the Galileans. This caused further conflict. These combined conditions created an ideal environment for unrest. Failure by the Zealots to correct the conditions led to an era of revolt against the Romans.

TABGHA

Tabgha is a lovely grove on the shore of the Sea of Galilee near Capernaum. It commemorates the place where Jesus appeared to His disciples after the Resurrection. It was here while fishing they saw the resurrected Jesus on the shore. It is called the Primacy of Peter because it is alleged that here Jesus and Peter had the interchange in which Jesus asked Peter if he loved Him.

It is also the place where the multiplication of the loaves and fishes is celebrated.

KORAZIM

At the northern end of the sea, two miles from Capernaum, was the village of Korazim, a sister city with Capernaum and Magala in the curse put on them by Jesus because of disbelief. The city was renowned for its ornate synagogue made of black basil stone. In it, carved from a single stone, was the Seat of Moses from which the Torah would have been read.

In fulfillment of the curse placed on it by Jesus, it was destroyed by an earthquake.

MOUNT OF BEATITUDES

The hillside rising from the shores near Capernaum is the lovely mount known as the Mount of Beatitudes. The Greek name for the place, *Eremos*, means solitary or uninhabited. The Church of the Beatitudes commemorates the teaching of the Sermon on the Mount. The octagon shape is a reminder of the eight Beatitudes. It was built in 1938 by an Italian Association to help Italian missionaries. The exact location of Jesus' teaching session isn't known, but this setting is an ideal site to celebrate the event. The view from the mountain is a panorama of the northern part of the Sea of Galilee and the Golan.

There are no quotation marks in Jesus' Sermon on the Mount. However, there is every reason to accept the text as a genuine representation of the message. It is likely Jesus preached the essence of the message on several occasions. After all, His audience was not static. The flow of traffic through the region expanded His congregants.

Jesus' manner of speaking is interesting. He taught seated as was the custom of a scribe. Often overlooked by speakers of the present generation, "He opened His mouth and taught them."

This reveals an elemental aspect of public speaking. It is essential to make sure the people can hear a clear, clarion voice.

At a time in the ministry of Jesus, He was perceived as a prophet who declared the end of the world and judgment. Those vital proclamations were augmented by Jesus in the Sermon on the Mount. His message was one espousing practical ethnical norms. It was a radical new worldview, a counter-cultural message calling for a new way of thinking and behaving. The title given the message, The Beatitudes, is not found in the Bible, but it is appropriate in that it means The Joys of Heaven, or a Declaration of Blessedness. And . . . very importantly, they are *be* attitudes and not *do* attitudes.

The eastern shore of the sea had much less activity recorded in Scripture, but that does not lessen the importance of the events there.

SHECHEM

Shechem's location in the valley between Mount Ebel and Mount Gerizim was a crossing point of three major highways. It was near the terminus of The Way of the Patriarchs, also called the Ridge Road, because it travels a vital mountain ridge through Jerusalem to Hebron.

From Ur, Abraham first crossed the Fertile Crescent to Shechem, the first city he came to in the land of promise. Here he built an altar to the Lord, and God confirmed His promise to give him the land.

Jacob, grandson of Abraham, was renamed Israel on the eastern side of the Jordan River at Jabok. He built an altar naming it El-eolhe-Israel, meaning God, the God of Israel (Genesis 33: 17 - 20). Becoming a herdsman, he dug a well for his large herds. One of his wells is still open in Shechem.

Years later, Jacob sent his seventeen-year-old son Joseph to

Shechem to visit his brothers who were tending the herds (Genesis 37: 12 - 14). Finding they had moved to greener pastures in Dothan, he went there to visit them. It was from there that Joseph's odyssey leading to his being prime minister of Egypt began.

Years later, Moses instructed the people to go to Shechem and pronounce the blessings and the curses of the Mosaic Covenant on the nation (Deuteronomy 27: 4). In doing so, Joshua divided the nation. Half of them stood in front of Mount Gerizim and half in front of Ebal. From Ebal, they shouted the curses of the law if they disobeyed, and from Mount Gerizim they shouted the blessings if they obeyed. Since that day, the two mountains have been known as the Mountain of Curses and the Mountain of Blessing.

Joshua's resounding charge was issued to the people of Shechem: "If it seem evil unto you to serve the Lord, choose for yourselves this day whom you will serve, whether the gods which your fathers served that were on the other side of the River, or the gods of the Amorites, in whose land you dwell. But as for me and my house, we will serve the Lord" (Joshua 24: 15).

After the passing of Saul, David, and Solomon, "Rehoboam went to Shechem, for all Israel had gone to Shecheum to make him king" (I Kings 12; 1). Rehoboam took the foolish advice of some of his youthful friends and divided the nation at Shechem into the ten northern tribes of the north from the southern kingdom of Judah (I Kings 12: 1 - 16).

Jeroboam made Shechem capital of the Northern Kingdom.

Jerusalem was the only designated place God established for worship. Since Jerusalem was in Judah, Jeroboam established a different place for worship in Shechem, complete with a golden bull. Thus, members of the northern tribes could worship without going into Judah. This idolatrous place was just south of Shechem where their forefathers and Joshua had made the covenant to worship God alone (I Kings 12: 25 - 33).

The people who worshiped on Mount Gerizim became known as Samaritans. There is a small colony of about three hundred

Samaritans who live in Shechem, now known as Nablus. They consider themselves the true guardians of the Law. Mount Gerizim, where the ancestors built their temple in the fourth century BC, is still their holy mountain. The temple was destroyed by the Judean king Hyrcanus in 128 BC.

These Samaritans claim to have the oldest Torah (the Pentateuch, or first five books of Moses) in existence. They allege Abisha, the great-grandson of Aaron, wrote it thirteen years after the Israelites conquered Canaan, making it over three thousand years old.

Of all the meaningful responses at Shechem, the moment the people were called upon by Joshua to serve the Lord is paramount: "We will serve the Lord...the Lord God we will serve, and His voice we will obey" (Joshua 24: 21, 24).

SAMARIA

Omri, king of the northern kingdom of Israel, who reigned 884 BC to 873 BC, purchased an oblong hill with a long flat top from Shemer and built his new capital thereon. He gave it the name Shomron, that is, Samaria.

Archaeologists believe Samaria was the richest and most developed city in all Israel or Judah.

Samaria, in addition to being the name of the capital city, is the name also associated with the central region of the biblical land of Israel.

In 30 BC, Emperor Augustus awarded the city to Herod the Great who renamed it Sebaste.

The transitions from Assyrian to Babylonian rule, from Babylonian to Persian rule, and from Persian to Hellenistic rule were, on the whole, relatively peaceful in the southern Levant. Although there was a major Samaritan revolt against Alexander the Great, which was put down with the utmost brutality, there is no indication it resulted in the destruction of Samaria itself.

Of the numerous times Samaria was attacked, the assault by Ben Hadad II against Ahab was among the most significant. Thirty-two vassal kings were aligned with Ben Hadad II; nevertheless, he was defeated with a great slaughter (I Kings 20: 1 - 21). The next year he made another futile assault and, when routed, was forced to surrender to Ahab, whose army by size was like "two little flocks of kids" (I Kings 20: 28 - 34).

During the rule of Hoshea, the last king of the Northern Kingdom, the Assyrians invaded in 722 BC. Upon conquering the city, the Assyrians gained control of the entire region. According to an inscription in Sargon's palace at Khorsab, Assyria, the inhabitants of Samaria were deported to Assyria. This was the end of the Northern Kingdom.

Philip, the Evangelist, preached and healed the sick in Samaria. This was the first successful evangelical effort outside of Jerusalem. Among the respondents was Simon Magnus, a highly influential man, who practiced sorcery. With his magic, he had made many followers. When he heard Philip preach, he responded. Thereafter he contended with Philip, trying to deceive people with his sorcery, but he soon realized Philip was for real. Peter and John, upon hearing of the converts, came to Samaria. After they shared further with the new believers, the Holy Spirit came upon them. Simon offered to pay Peter and John for the power to do as they did. They sternly rebuked him for thinking the power of the Holy Spirit was something to be purchased. His response was not favorable.

In the first century, in extra-biblical sources, the Church Fathers began to write of Simon Magnus, depicting him as the arch-heretic of Christianity, the father of all heresies. He is credited with having founded the greatest heresy of the era, Gnosticism.

Samaria was where Jesus met the woman at Jacob's well and revealed himself to be the Messiah. It was also the home of the legendary Good Samaritan.

John the Baptist is believed to be buried in Samaria. In August 362, Roman emperor Julian ordered the destruction of the tomb of

John the Baptist and the cremation of the remains. A small basilica church found in the fifth century is believed to be the burial place of the head of John the Baptist.

In 333 BC, Alexander the Great conquered Judah from the Persians and included it in his empire. The Greeks dominated the territory of the old state of Israel from 333 BC until the late 160s BC. He Hellenized the entire region, including the language.

KURSI

Three Gospels tell the story of Jesus being here. In going to this region, Jesus was obviously in Gentile country. Swine were taboo among the Jews who had laws forbidding the keeping of unclean animals (Leviticus 11: 7). When Jesus stepped out of a boat after crossing the lake, He was confronted by two fierce men possessed by demons. Upon being ordered by Jesus to leave the men, the demons begged to be allowed to enter a herd of swine feeding nearby. Jesus agreed, and the swine—numbering about two thousand— "rush down a bank into the water and are drowned" (Luke 8:26-39; Mark 5:1-20; Matthew 8:28-34).

The swine-keepers went into the city and told the people what happened, including the deliverance of themselves. Sitting on the Golan Heights above the community of Kursi was the city of Hippos, one of the cities of the Decapolis. Being the nearest city, it is likely the city being described. In their recounting of their being healed, they must have emphasized their economic loss rather than the healing because when the people saw Jesus, "They begged Him to depart from their region" (Matthew 5: 34).

Matthew and Mark differ in recording the incident. Matthew reports there being two possessed men and does not mention one going into the city, while Mark reports only one possessed man and he went into the city. This is not a conflict. Matthew was writing to a Jewish audience which requires two witnesses to verify an event, so he gave more details and reports on both men. If there were two men, it is logical there was one. Mark simply emphasizes the action of one of them. This is a confirmation there was no collusion by the gospel writers.

DAN

Dan was a prominent Old Testament city in the Upper Galilee region of the Hula Valley. It was the northernmost of the cities of the Kingdom of Israel. It is located at the foot of Mount Hermon, near Mount Lebanon. Melting snow from the summits provides the water of the Dan River which flows through Dan helping to form the Jordan River, which feeds into the Sea of Galilee.

Two golden calves were used for worship. One was fashioned there by Rehoboam. The other was at Bethel.

The first ancient inscription outside the Bible bearing David's name was found recently in Dan. Dated from the ninth century, it bears the inscription *House of David* and *King of Israel*. The phrase *House of David* indicates it refers, not just to David, but to the dynasty of David.

BEERSHEBA

Though located some distance from Dan at the other end of Israel, Beersheba is a city often associated with it. The colloquialism was "from Dan to Beersheba" which spoke of all the land of Israel. It is located about fifty miles south of Jerusalem.

Abraham offered hospitality to the three strangers at nearby Mamre near Hebron who told him his ninety-year-old wife Sara would have a son (Genesis 18: 10 - 14).

Located in Hebron in the Cave of Machpelah are the Tombs of the Patriarchs: Abraham and Sarah, Isaac and Rebekah, and Jacob and Leah.

About seven hundred years after Abraham, Moses sent spies into this area who returned with a cluster of grapes that were so large they had to be carried on a pole between them. This has subsequently become the symbol of the Israeli Ministry of Tourism.

HAZOR

Hazor, one of the largest and most strategically located biblical sites, was on the main highway between Egypt in the south and Mesopotamia in the north. It was a valued military target by many armies but was controlled principally by the Canaanites and Israel. The story of Hazor is one of several milestone events in the history of the land:

- One historically significant event was an attempt to halt Joshua's conquest of the land. King Jabin of Hazor led a coalition of five Canaanite city-states which gathered at the Waters of Merom to fight against Joshua. Hazor is described as "the head of all those nations" (Joshua 11: 10, 11). Its military force consisted of "as many as the sand that is on the seashore in multitude, with very many horses and chariots" (Joshua 11: 4). Joshua defeated Jabin and returned to Hazor and burned the city.
- A second involved the Canaanites' rebuilding the city, enabling it to once more emerge as a powerful force. Under the leadership of their renowned leader Sisera, they undertook the conquest of Israeli territory. In the battle near Mount Tabor, his army was defeated by the forces of the prophetess Deborah's great general Barak (Judges 4:2).
- The third event occurred during the days of the United Monarchy when Solomon once more fortified Hazor and rebuilt the walls (I Kings 9:15). The prestige of the city was restored. With their new status, the people became arrogant and distant from the Lord. Through the prophets, God warned the people to humble themselves or God would humble them with a great earthquake (Amos 1: 2ff). In 1950, archaeological evidence emerged indicating that an earthquake measuring 8.2 on the Richter scale devastated the city, leaving it in ruins in the mid eighth century BC.
- The fourth catastrophic event involved the Northern Kingdom

of Israel failing to heed the warning of Amos regarding a great judgment to come on them if they did not repent. Failing to do so, the judgment came in the form of an Assyrian invasion in 732 BC by King Toglath-Pileser III of Assyria.

Israel's failure to respond to its repeated devastation, both by military and natural forces, resulted in the nation being taken into captivity (Leviticus 26: 32-39). Archeologists have uncovered evidence of their disobedience beneath the Assyrian destruction strata. They found partially eaten pig indicating Israel's disobedience of the Mosaic Law prohibiting the eating of pork (Isaiah 65: 1-4; Leviticus 11: 7).

CAESAREA PHILLIPI

Alexander the Great conquered the region and from here started his Hellenization of Egypt and Syria. A city of Panias was established, the name of which became Banias. Panias was named for the Greek god Pan, half man and half goat, known for his flute. It was said when he was in a good mood, his music was beautiful and soothing. When he was upset or distraught, his music was erratic and disturbing. Such conduct gave us the word *panic*.

The area is also known as Caesarea Phillipi, not to be confused with Caesarea Maritima, the Caesarea by the Mediterranean. The city is referenced in both Matthew and Mark.

Though Jesus ministered and taught in the area, there is no indication He entered the city. The setting, however, was the ideal for one of His best teaching moments. A small red mountain with an open face had in it a cave from which a stream flowed. Therein was an altar to Pan around which cultic worship occurred. Jesus' interchange with Peter at Banias is best understood in light of the time (Matthew 16: 13 - 19).

After Peter confessed Jesus to be "the Christ, the Son of the Living God," Jesus replied, "On this rock I will build my church, and the gates of Hades shall not prevail against it. And I will give you the keys of the kingdom of heaven, and whatever you bind on earth will be bound in heaven, and whatever you loose on earth will be loosed in heaven" (Matthew 16: 18, 19).

With this large red rock mountain as a backdrop, Jesus asked Peter who He was. An interchange ensued resulting in Jesus saying, "You are Peter and upon this rock I will build my church" (Matthew 16: 13 - 19).

Peter had answered Jesus' initial inquiry by saying, "You are the Christ, the Son of the Living God" (vs. 16).

Jesus' retort was, "You are Peter (Petros), and on this rock (Petra) I will build my church (vs. 18). The play on words is more than play.

Petros used as a reference to Simon Peter referred to a small stone which could easily be moved. Peter's vacillating personality later verified the validity of this moniker.

Petra meant a large unmovable rock, a mountain-like Gibraltar with a large subsurface mass. It was used by Jesus as referring to the confession made by Peter: "the Christ, the Son of the Living God." Jesus, Who is the living embodiment of that statement, is the foundation on which the church rests.

In the biblical era when Jerusalem had a threat, the elders of the city would gather at the gates of the city to plot and plan what to do. In this expression Jesus showed resolute determination by, in effect, saying, "I will build my church. Let the devil and all the demons of hell get together to strategize how to prevent me, and they can't."

Then followed another strategic part of their interchange when Jesus spoke of the keys of the kingdom of heaven. In that era, young rabbis studied from older rabbis. The older rabbi would have a key to the cabinet in which the scroll, the Word of God, was kept locked. He was the keeper of the key to the cabinet containing the scroll. He would open the cabinet, remove the scroll, and teach the young rabbi the lesson of the moment. Then he would return the scroll and lock the cabinet. When the young rabbi had learned all the lessons necessary and "graduated," he was given a key allowing him to open the cabinet, take out the scroll, and interpret it for the people that they might understand and apply it.

Peter had been with Jesus, his rabbi, and learned the lessons taught well enough to know Jesus was "the Christ, the Son of the Living God." He was now entitled to share the lesson.

Jesus' comments regarding the keys are to be understood in light of the sharing of the gospel. It meant that if the Word of God is unlocked and loosed, that is, applied, the power of Heaven would be engaged in its sharing. If the cabinet, that is, the Word, is kept bound, locked up, there is no power of heaven to loose it, thereby enabling people to understand and live it. In summary, the passage is an instruction to learn the Word in order to share it with the confidence God will empower it. The Word becomes alive and powerful when unlocked and shared.

Contrary to current conduct, this is not license to pray a prayer "binding Satan" in a given area or time.

MOUNT CARMEL

Mount Carmel is not a mountain, but a part of the coastal range. It is often cited in Scripture for its beauty and fertility. It has long been considered a special spiritual place to which, at one time, people were forbidden to go. It affords a magnificent view of the plain of Esdraelon, known as the Valley of Armageddon.

The southeast summit of Mount Carmel was the setting for the dramatic confrontation between Elijah's God and the pagan god Baal. The confrontation occurred after a succession of kings "did evil in the sight of the Lord" (I Kings 16:30).

The face-off came at the time of a great drought. The purpose was two-fold. One was to pray for rain, and the other to test and prove the deities. It involved the priests of Baal praying for Baal to consume an altar, prepared for the occasion by fire. Upon the failure of Baal to act, Elijah had water poured on the altar, and he called upon God to consume it with fire. He did, thus exposing the fraudulent character of Baal.

So impressed are most people with God raining down fire that a major point is missed. The great need at the time was for water. When Elijah poured water on the altar, he was sacrificing to God the most precious thing he had.

MOUNT HERMON

Mount Hermon, the northern-most point of Joshua's conquest of the Promised Land, is located on the border between Israel, Lebanon, and Syria. The highest of its twin peaks is more than nine thousand feet above sea level. Snowmelt from the peaks provides a source of the waters of the Jordan River which flows through the Sea of Galilee and down the Jordan Valley to the Dead Sea. Reference is made to it in Scripture: (Joshua 11: 3, 17; 12: 1, 5; Psalms 42: 6; 89: 12; 133: 3; Song of Solomon.) It is considered to be one of the potential sites of the Transfiguration of Jesus' (Matthew 17: 1 - 9; Mark 9: 2 - 9; Luke 9: 28 - 37).

GAMLA

Gamla is located on a camel-back ridge framed by deep gorges of the Gamly and Daliyot streams. Obscured on the Golan Heights, it is reached only by one footpath on the northeast corner. It was first settled in the Early Bronze Age and later abandoned for a long period. It was once more inhabited by exiles from Babylon. Still later, Herod the Great settled Jews there to repopulate the area.

In 66 AD, the inhabitants reinforced the eastern wall, the only vulnerable part of the fortifications.

Earlier, the founder of the Zealot movement, Judas of Gamla, led a revolt against the Romans. The spirit of revolution birthed here infected the land, leading to the Jewish Revolt that led to the Zealots' destruction.

A member of the Sanhedrin, Gamaliel, noted this: "After this man, Judas of Galilee rose up in the days of the census, and drew away many people after him. He also perished, and all who obeyed him were dispersed" Acts 6: 37).

King Herod Antipas, controller of the Galilee, unsuccessfully besieged the city for seven months. Roman General Vespasian then laid siege to the city for a month during which he suffered significant casualties. Finally, the Romans breached the wall near the synagogue. The city had been flooded by refugees fleeing the Romans. Reacting to the onslaught of the Romans, nine thousand people took their own lives by jumping from cliffs. General Josephus escaped from here and went on to become the chronicler of the Roman campaigns in Israel.

The synagogue is the oldest one known in Israel, dating from the early first century.

JORDAN RIVER

The Jordan River is mentioned a hundred and seventy-five times in the Old Testament and fifteen times in the New Testament. The root meaning of the name means to *descend*. It is appropriate in that the waters descend from Mount Hermon, elevation more than nine thousand feet feet, to the Dead Sea, fourteen hundred feet below sea level, resulting in it being one of the fastest flowing streams in the world.

On a straight line, it is forty miles from the summit of Mount Hermon to the Sea of Galilee, and from there to the Dead Sea it is less than seventy miles, giving it a length of approximately one hundred and ten miles. Its circuitous route is nearly two hundred and twenty miles.

Most of the year near the mouth of the Jordan River at the Dead Sea, the temperature is approximately 25 to 35 degrees centigrade. At flood, it is often a mile wide. It was flood time when the Children of Israel crossed into the Promised Land.

Jesus was baptized in the Jordan. The site regarded as the most likely place is on the Jordan River, known as Al-Maghtas. On the Israeli west bank, it is known as Bethabara, meaning, house of the ford. The gospel writers posture the site as near the wilderness at a place accessible to Jerusalem. John is represented as having been "preaching in the wilderness of Judea" and "people from Jerusalem, all of Judea, and all the region around the Jordan went out to him.... Then Jesus came from Galilee to the Jordan to John, to be baptized by him" (Matthew 3: 13).

These details discredit the lovely site near the end of the Sea of Galilee often used by tourists being baptized in the Jordan. It is an inviting site for reverence.

At Bethabara (Al-Maghtas), the river is muddy and the banks overgrown with reeds, tamarisk, and willows, making it less scenic than the northern site near the Sea of Galilee.

In various cultures, rivers are highly regarded and thought of as a source of blessing. By the ancient Hebrews, it was looked upon as an obstacle to be overcome. "To cross the Jordan" became an idiom for success, overcoming an obstacle. For that reason, the river is often looked upon as a foreboding obstacle to be overcome.

The hymn "I Won't Have to Cross Jordan Alone" speaks of God helping persons overcoming obstacles.

GIDEON SPRING

En Harod is identified with Gideon (Judges 7) and two mighty men of David (II Samuel 23: 25). The name means Spring of Trembling. The waters flow from the spring of Harod, a cave at the base of Mount Gilboa in the Jazreel Valley. Here Gideon camped the night before his encounter with the Midianites.

Gideon conducted his final tests at the spring, reducing his army from thirty-two thousand to only three hundred warriors (Judges 7: 1 - 7). His small force could see the hundred thirty-five thousand Midianite army on the hills of Moreh. Against the odds of four hundred fifty to one, Gideon faced down his fears and trusted God for the victory He had promised.

Through the ages, this has been the site where armies have marshaled for battle or engaged in warfare. In one such battle fought in 1260, Baybars I, a Mameluke general, defeated the Mongolian army that had invaded the land. This was the final battle ending the Mongolian occupation in the Middle East.

JERICHO

Jericho, ten miles north of the Dead Sea, is reputed to be the oldest continually inhabited place on earth, dating back to 9,000 BC. At eight hundred and forty-six feet below sea level, it is also the lowest inhabited place on earth.

Long believed to have very special characteristics, Jericho was a gift to the Egyptian Queen Cleopatra from Mark Anthony in 35 BC. She desired it because of a persimmon tree, now extinct, that produced a perfume which allegedly "drove men wild."

The formidable walls of Jericho made its conquest by Joshua all the more remarkable.

In the New Testament, Jesus is pictured in Matthew 18: 29-34 and Mark 10: 46-52 as leaving Jericho, while Luke 18: 35-43 portrays Him as going to Jericho.

The apparent conflict is resolved by there being two Jerichos. Jesus was leaving the old uninhabited Jericho of Joshua's day, and Luke is referring to the Roman Jericho of the New Testament era. The healing reported as having occurred was on the road between the two cities.

Today, the present city is further south of the old Jericho. There are three Jerichos, the current city and the remains of the two former ones.

EIN GEDI

Ein Gedi, one of the most popular nature sites in Israel, is an oasis on the shores of the Dead Sea between Masada and Qumran.

Biblically, it is identified as the stronghold of Ein Gedi where David hid from King Saul (I Samuel 23: 29; 24: 1,2). Saul is depicted as searching for him "even upon the most craggy rocks, which are accessible only to wild goats" (I Samuel 24: 2). Ein Gedi has been associated with the description of David in the wilderness of Psalm 63. The caves in the area hint of the ideal nature for one being hunted to hide.

The modern-day park includes two spring-fed streams that flow all year. The falls they produce are pictorial. Two other springs also provide water for the arid region.

Among the plants along the streams are Sodom apple, acacia, jujuba, and poplar. Nubian ibex are numerous in the area. A variety of species of birds reside in the region. Their numbers are swollen by over two hundred species of migratory birds.

QUMRAN

Qumran is a historical site about one mile from the northwest shore of the Dead Sea. It was here the first of the Dead Sea Scrolls were found in the sheer cliffs and the marl terrace. The discovery of these ancient scrolls, beginning in 1947, has aided in the understanding of the period in which they were written. Since 1967, the scrolls have been housed in the Shrine of the Book museum in Jerusalem.

The first settlement here was during the Hellenistic period, and it remained inhabited until the Roman period. When the people saw the Romans were coming, they hid their Holy Books in the caves and fled.

The remains of the Jewish monastic community have shown them to have been a self-sufficient and isolated society. There has been much mystery and debate about the colony with many answers still needed. The inhabitants are believed to have been Essenes. In compliance with the Manual of Discipline in the Dead Sea Scrolls, they were fastidiously clean and dietetically well disciplined. This may have contributed to their downfall.

The population is variously estimated to have ranged from as low as twelve to fifteen and then as high as a hundred fifty to two hundred males only. Their great hall would seat a hundred and fifty people. There were a thousand dishes in the pantry. It is thought by some that John the Baptist was among their numbers for a time.

Amid the numerous buildings were several fresh-water cisterns and several ritual baths. The hygienic habits of the residents called for them to go to a nearby valley to use it as a toilet area. Upon returning, they would engage in ritual bathing. One hypothesis is that bacteria brought back from the toilet area contaminated the ritual bath waters, which led to the eventual annihilation of the colony.

THE DEAD SEA SCROLLS

Eleven caves near the Qumran settlement provided most of the writings known as the Dead Sea Scrolls. Other caves also provided scrolls. They consist of numerous religious and secular writings. About two hundred and thirty are considered biblical scrolls. Scrolls range in date from the third century BC to the first century. Some of the scrolls are more than a thousand years older than previously identified biblical manuscripts.

MASADA

The plateau fortress of Masada rises a thousand three hundred feet above the Judean sands south of En Gedi on the western shore of the Dead Sea. Its rhomboid plateau is approximately a half mile long. Among the palaces, storage barns, bathhouses, residences, and the synagogue, there was space for growing crops. To strengthen its defensibility, in addition to the height of the cliffs supporting it, a casement was erected around the perimeter of the summit. An intricate system for collecting and storing water was developed.

Masada, meaning strong foundation, was first established in the second century BC, and finished as one of the fortress palaces of Herod the Great between 37 and 4 BC. The summit was reached by a narrow winding snake path which climbs nine hundred feet.

In 66, a group known as Sicarii, led by Eleazar ben Yair, came to the Galilee at the beginning of a revolt. The fortress was, in effect, to withstand the Romans. Masada became one of the last fortress holdouts against the Romans.

Many debate whether, in the years 72 -73, the Roman Legion Tenth Fretensis, under the command of Flavius Silva, lay siege to ben Yair's fortress in an effort to end the rebellion. The nine thousand Roman soldiers plus their support personnel and slaves employed most tactics used in siege warfare. Often a show of force would motivate a city or fortress to surrender. As a show of force and to give an indication of how long they were willing to continue the siege, the Romans built eight large encampments at strategic locations. A six-foot-thick, seven-mile-long circumvallation wall was built around the base to isolate the fortress. Roman catapults hurled large stones over the walls of Masada.

Slowly, Jews, who were Roman slaves, built an earthen ramp on the western side. The Romans were correct in their belief the defending Jews would not fire on the Jews building the ramp, though it led to the Jews' demise. A battering ram was designed to be moved up the ramp and thus began the process of breaching the wall.

Stories vary regarding the last hours of the holdout. Most commonly it is believed that Eleazer ben Yair, the rebel leader, convinced the nine hundred sixty inhabitants that death was preferable to Roman slavery, and they took their own lives. Ten men were selected to kill everyone else, including women and children. One of them then killed the nine and himself. Based on the lack of human remains at the site, the account of mass suicide is being questioned. Remains of only twenty persons have been found and only three in the place Josephus reported the mass killing to have occurred.

According to Josephus, what happened was reported by two women and five children who hid and avoided the slaughter.

Based on recent studies by geologist Dan Gill of the Geological Survey of Israel, there are discrepancies in Josephus' account. An example is the earthen ramp used by the Romans. Gill alleges the ramp was not a Roman marvel but was built on a narrow spur sloping at about twenty degrees descending from about forty feet below the top of the western approach of Masada. This spur forms the base for layers of man-made earthwork overlaying it. He avers the spur is a natural topographical feature consisting of almost nine million feet of earth. The Roman overlay completing the ramp averaged twenty-six feet thick. Geologically, the mass of earthwork is not jumbled rock and loosened earth, but local bedrock. Near the top of the ramp and at intervals along the sides, the bedrock can now be distinguished from the man-made fill.

The dimensions of the ramp have been calculated to have been fifty feet wide, twenty-six feet deep, and five hundred and ten feet long, giving a total volume for the man-made portion of the ramp of approximately six hundred thousand cubic feet. Based on the calculations by Gill, the mass of the man-made part of the ramp could have been constructed in as little as eight days by eight hundred men working in three shifts twenty-four hours a day, each providing thirty-five cubic feet of fill per day.

Additionally, features and details included in his study indicate the construction of the staging apparatus and execution of the siege would have required only between four and seven months.

HERODIUM

The imposing Herodium was built by Herod the Great as one of his fortress palaces. It stands out on the horizon and gives an impressive view of Judean hills and desert as well as the Mountains of Moab in the distance.

According to Josephus, Herod built it in 20 BC on the spot where he won his decisive victory over the Hasmonean and Parthian enemies.

The complex was built in two distinctive areas. The circular fortress, including the opulent palace, sits atop the man-made mountain surrounded by walls and towers. Herod devised the concept of building a palace within a fortress. Though comparatively small, the palace was sumptuously appointed, giving evidence of an opulent lifestyle with all the creature comforts of the time.

The fortress was originally built to the height of a seven-story building. This ninety-eight-foot outer wall with seven towers was separated by several feet from a less imposing inner wall. Later, a large landfill covered the walls all around the outside. Dirt was brought in from nearby hills.

Water was brought through canals from springs near Bethlehem called Solomon's pools. An additional source was provided by rainwater being drained into cisterns beneath the fortress. Additionally, three large cisterns were dug into the slope of the hill outside the fortress. Servants carried this water to the cisterns at the top of the hill which enabled them to stay full.

A number of underground passages and chambers permeate the core of the mountain that were designed as hiding places when the people were besieged.

On the plain to the north at the base of the hill, Herod built an administrative center for the territory on thirty-eight acres. It was centered around a large pool seventy-six yards by fifty yards. Water was brought to the pool by way of an aqueduct from the springs at Artas near Solomon's Pool.

After the Roman destruction of Jerusalem, Herodium and Masada were the last holdouts in Israel by the Jews in opposition to the Roman conquest of 71. A large procession preceded the burial of Herod in a tomb he prepared for himself. The location of his tomb is still questionable.

HEBRON

Located in the Judean hills twenty miles southwest of Jerusalem is the oldest Jewish community in the world, Hebron. It is one of the oldest continually inhabited communities in the world. Abraham purchased the site, including the Cave of Machpelah, from

Ephron the Hittite for a burial place for his wife Sarah. Thus, it became the first parcel of land owned by a Jew in the Promised Land. According to Jewish tradition, the Patriarchs Abraham, Isaac, and Jacob, along with the Matriarchs Sarah, Rebecca, and Leah, are buried here. The Byzantines built a large church over the burial cave.

In Hebron, three angels of the Lord visited the ninety-nine year-old Abraham and told him his wife Sarah would bear a son one year later.

When Moses sent twelve spies into the land, one of them, Caleb, went to the tombs of the Patriarchs to pray he would not fall victim to the wicked plot of his colleagues.

When Joshua conquered the land, it was given him.

David was anointed King of Israel here and ruled from here for seven years.

Tradition also holds Adam and Eve are buried in Hebron.

GEZER

"Pharaoh King of Egypt had attacked and captured Gezer ... and Solomon rebuilt Gezer" (I Kings 9:17). This speaks of the turbulence of the city. Pharaoh captured it and later gave it to Solomon as a part of his daughter's dowry when she became one of Solomon's wives. Solomon fortified the city and even stored his chariots there. A layer of debris from 950 BC, a date coinciding with the Egyptian conquest, has been found.

Nomads camped in the area for years before a small contingency settled there around 4000 BC. In the middle Bronze Age (circa 1500 BC), the imposing city on the edge of the Coastal Plain midway between Tel Aviv and Jerusalem was surrounded by massive walls and towers. It served as a guardian of the primary route from Egypt to Jerusalem. It is considered to have been one of the most important cities of the Canaanite era. From its elevation the expansive Aijalon Valley can be viewed.

Today's archaeological discoveries feature monumental

columns from one of the largest Canaanite temples in the land as well as the Solomonic gate. Also carved in the limestone is one of the largest water tunnels in Israel.

Among the most intriguing finds was the Gezer Calendar, one of the earliest known examples of Hebrew writing. The calendar lists the eight periods of the agricultural year and tasks associated with each.

A row of unique standing stones, *stelae*, remain from what is believed to have been the center of Canaanite religious culture. They mark a colonnaded ritual site. Large assemblies were held here by members from Canaanite cities as a show of unity.

Jars containing the remains of infants have been found which give support to the belief Canaanites practiced infant sacrificing. Some contend they are only infants that died from natural causes and were buried near their gods.

Outstanding present-day archaeological discoveries in Gezer tend to redefine some ancient timelines.

LACHISH

The earliest remains at Tel Lachish belong to the Neolithic period (8300 - 4500 BC). The ancient fortress city was located in south-central Israel between Mount Hebron and the Mediterranean coast. It was a fortress town designed to protect Jerusalem. Of the sieges of Lachish, the one by the Assyrian King Sennacherib in 701 BC stands out. Several kingdoms in the area had ceased paying taxes, so the king set out to once again subjugate the inhabitants.

The walled city was built on a steep hill and well fortified. The Jewish army, which consisted of local militia and mercenaries, was vastly inferior to the besieging Assyrian forces. Assyrian engineers built a ramp to the east of the main gate up which they brought siege engines and broke the wall, thus conquering the city.

Inhabitants were led into captivity and their leaders tortured to death. Lachish was then used as the base from which the Assyrians laid siege on Jerusalem.

At a later period following the return of the Israelites from the Babylonian captivity, the city was inhabited again. Hezekiah, the twelfth king of Judea, was the devout son of his godless father, Ahaz. Upon ascending to the throne, Hezekiah sought to rid the land of idolatry by ordering all false deities and idols worshipped in the land to be destroyed.

In recent years, archaeologists have found evidence of his war against idolatry. A towering gate and shrine dating from the eighth century BC is believed to be a place where false worship occurred. The horns of the altar had been cut off, giving evidence it was destroyed as a place of worship.

In the corner of the shrine was found a toilet. The Bible describes other occasions on which toilets were placed in cultic areas in order to desecrate them. For example, it is noted Jehu did so in Samaria (II Kings 10: 27).

In the time of Joshua, the king of Lachish aligned with four other kings, confronted Joshua in the battle of Gibeon, which Joshua won. All five kings were executed.

Joshua attacked Lachish, and "the Lord delivered Lachish into the hand of Israel, who took it on the second day..." (Joshua 10: 32).

JAFFA

Present-day Jaffa is primarily an art colony built over the original city. It claims to be the oldest seaport in the world. The oldest remains are sun-dried bricks dating from the sixteenth century BC.

The Zodiac alleys are a maze of restored passageways leading to the harbor. Jaffa Hill is a center for archaeological finds, including restored Egyptian gates, about thirty-five hundred years old. These features combined with the ornate homes and large plaza make for an ideal arts community.

It is believed to have been named for Jepheth, son of Noah.

Some consider it to have been given the Canaanite name *Yafi*, meaning beautiful.

The tel of Jaffa rises a hundred and thirty feet above the sea, affording a beautiful view of the coastline. Archaeological evidence indicates the city was settled in 7500 BC. It has been conquered twenty-two times. Perhaps its most unusual conquest was by the Egyptian Pharaoh Thurmoses III, who hid warriors in large baskets and gave them as gifts to the Canaanite occupants who, upon taking them in, were overwhelmed by the soldiers.

In the Middle Ages it was the only port from which pilgrims coming from Europe could dock. From here, the prophet Jonah set forth on his venture of being swallowed by a great fish (Jonah 1: 3). Cedars were rafted here from Lebanon to be used in the construction of Solomon's Temple (II Chronicles 2: 16).

Peter experienced his vision of a great sheet descending with a variety of animals in it. Upon hearing a heavenly voice telling him to eat, Peter refused, declaring he would not eat anything unclean. Again, the voice spoke, "What God has cleansed you must not call common" (Acts 10:15). Peter immediately saw the parallel regarding Jews letting Gentiles enter the church. In response to the invitation brought to him from Cornelius in Capernaum, Peter met with Cornelius, and he became the first known Gentile convert.

Though there is no actual connection to Bible sites, the lore of the city is rich. One site is represented as the location of the tomb of Tabitha, or in Greek *Dorcas*, who was raised from the dead by Peter (Acts 9: 36 -43). Another site is alleged to be the location of the home of Simon the Tanner, which is the rooftop where Peter received his vision. His vision is commemorated at Saint Peter's Church.

THE LANGUAGE AND THE LORE

The middle eastern mind is given to the use of colorful speech. Metaphors, symbols, and illustrations were popular manners of communication. An understanding of this mindset helps in the comprehension of what is meant.

Over the years the Greek-Roman thought pattern has obscured the meaning of some Scripture. Greek thinkers introduced abstract thought into interpretation. This thought is divorced from the facts of the here and now. Jesus met people where they were and related relevant truths.

Knowing people tend to think in pictures and relate to stories, Jesus used such as His platform for communicating. The eastern mind was visual and contingent on circumstances. Jesus used word-pictures to illustrate eternal truths. He made elevated thought understandable to the average citizen.

Lacking a Hebrew pattern of thought, we tend to interpret Scripture in light of our environment and experience. The better we see Scripture in the context of its time of origin, the better we can comprehend it. Learning to interact with Scripture on such a level makes it more understandable and relevant.

Communication involves two parties, the one sending the message and the one receiving it. Often the two come from different backgrounds and use different styles of communication. The western mind tends to basically think from a logical standpoint. The eastern mind is given to using metaphor, figurative colorful speech that is illustrative. An example of these two methods is Jesus' account of the lilies of the field: "Consider the lilies of the field, how they grow: they neither toil or spend; and yet I say to you that even Solomon in all his glory was not arrayed like one of these" (Matthew 6: 29, 30).

The critical, logical western mind might say lilies aren't clothed, and if God loved Solomon more than the lilies, why did He clothe them better than Solomon?

The eastern mind more easily accepts this as figurative speech, using metaphors and analogies to encourage people to rely on God providing for them so that there will be no reason to worry. To the eastern reader the clothing is metaphoric. To the western mind the clothes are literal clothes.

In general, three areas of knowledge existed in the Bible era. What Jesus said regarding each needs to be understood in light of what He meant, not just what we think.

Government was an essential and popular area. Jesus spoke very seldomly of it. He did say, "Render unto Caesar that which is Caesar's and unto God that which is God's" (Matthew 22: 21). Likewise, Jesus said to Pilate, "You could have no authority at all against Me unless it had been given you from above" (John 19: 10).

Economy was a second area of knowledge. Again, comparatively He spoke little about it. He encouraged giving freely (Matthew 10: 8), and discouraged hoarding (Matthew 6: 19, 20).

Knowledge was the area in which He asserted Himself. "He taught them as one having authority, and not as the scribes" (Matthew 7: 29). The scribes quoted one another and various sources but did not teach creatively. He frequently said, "You have heard it said, but I say to you...," asserting His authority. It was said of Him that "never a man spoke like this" (John 7: 46). Scripture repeatedly speak of Jesus' knowledge and authority:

- At His birth it was said, "He was filled with wisdom" (Luke 2: 40).
- Of His youth it was noted, "Jesus increased in wisdom" (Luke 2: 52).
- Observers concluded, "He spoke with authority and power" (Luke 4: 36).
- Summarily, He concluded by saying, "All authority is given unto me in heaven and on earth..." (Matthew 28: 18).

After hearing Him, his listeners asked, "Where did this man get this wisdom?" (Matthew 13: 54). His knowledge and wisdom were the main things for which He was held in contempt and why He was eventually condemned.

Out of His vast repository of knowledge, He shared His heavenly mind with all.

THE HUMOR OF JESUS

The language makes for the laugh. What constitutes humor varies over time. What was humorous twenty years ago hardly gets a smile today. Every language has its standard for what is humorous today, as it was in the era of the Bible. There are various kinds of humor: irony, hyperbole, embellishment, overstatement, and simple wit. Jesus used most of these forms.

The humor of Jesus' time was so subtle that it is often overlooked today. Yet, He used it to teach, to heal, and to evangelize. He did so in such a way as not to distract from its intended end. The nuances in His style make it all the more appealing. His well-crafted nuances, word play, irony, and timing enriched His messages. His style was that of His day. The common and elite could understand His intended message. Encasing it at times in humorous ways, they knew, aided in its understanding. Jesus' humor was not an end in itself, but a means to an end.

Humor is such a good communication tool and affords such therapy, why should He not use it? God encouraged Nehemiah not to be overly somber saying, "The joy of the Lord is your strength" (Nehemiah 8: 10). The therapeutic advantage of humor is seen in the assurance that "a merry heart does good like a medicine" (Proverbs 17: 22). Jesus Himself exhorted His followers to "be of good cheer," saying there is good reason for good cheer: "I have overcome the world" (John 16: 33).

He used humor to break down barriers and stimulate thought. By it, His audience was able to see Him more fully and understand Him more clearly. There must have been at least a snicker among the apostles when Jesus called the vacillating Peter the "Rock." That is like calling a person who is seven feet tall "Shorty."

The hypocritical, pretentious, bigoted religious leaders of the day were perfect foils for His wit. They never saw anything humorous about what He said, being blinded by their rigid aloofness and self-righteousness.

The idea of the blind leading the blind evoked a humorous image of helplessness (Matthew 15: 14). What a silly thing to do, putting a lamp under a bushel or especially a bed (Mark 4:21). Hearers envisioning a camel trying to go through the eye of a needle would consider the scene ludicrously funny (Mark 10: 25).

Gestures and facial expressions certainly would have added to the words to interpret what was said, and Jesus surely had them.

The language variance between that of the Bible and today is a barrier to understanding Oriental humor. Jesus referred to a gnat and a camel in Matthew 23: 24. In the Aramaic language of the day, the word for gnat is *galma* and the word for camel is *gamla*. This wordplay is lost in the translation. The mental picture of a person trying to swallow a camel was humorous.

The parable of the unforgiving debtor (Matthew 18: 23 - 35) would have had a humorous twist in Jesus' day. He told of a slave who owed the king a lot of money, ten thousand talents. We miss the point not knowing that amount was more than the Roman government had. His audience would have known right away that is a lot. The plot thickens when the man is called to pay and he asks for more time to do so. There would be no way to pay such a debt. The king responds by forgiving the debtor. That is funny because no king of the day would do such a silly thing.

There is a twist in the plot. The slave goes away and finds someone who owes him money, a hundred denarii. That is equivalent to a month's pay. He egregiously threatens the debtor, demanding immediate pay and even choking him. To the contemporary audience, that is a silly story. However, in its day it would have been heard by an attentive audience. Once Jesus had the attention of His listeners, He made His point. How ridiculous it is to hold a grudge against a person when the king, our great God, has forgiven us so much.

There is reason to be confident Jesus had a sense of humor and laughed. Having been depicted as weeping, it is reasonable to assume He had the opposite emotion. Like us, He was fully man. God created us with a sense of humor; therefore, Jesus had such also. God the Father is depicted as laughing at the defiant nations (Ezekiel 23: 32). Of His enemies, it is said, "You O Lord, shall laugh at them" (Psalm 59: 8). He made Sarah laugh at the thought of having a son. He said, "There is a time to laugh" (Ecclesiastes 3: 4).

Humor is basic in human nature; therefore, it is reasonable that Jesus had a sense of humor. Lives are enriched by good humor and genuine religion, and Jesus had both.

THE SOCIAL STRUCTURE

The story of the societal order of the land of the Bible in Jesus' time is one of the superimposition of one culture on another, each overlapping the other. It had been for some time a diverse culture. Each had its own values, preferences, and traditions resulting in an antagonistic, even inimical, society. The land was a microcosm of the world around it. Like meteors in the dark sky, each blazed for a time and fed from history. However, each culture left its imprint on the society. Each inscribed its own meaning to places and events. Jesus stepped into this milieu, making Him in effect a man of the world, that is, one adapted to relate to all people.

Against the societal tapestry, Jesus painted word pictures using allegories, proverbs, and parables and drawing images from the land and culture. What He said was not always what was meant literally. It was often symbolical, figurative, colloquial, and illustrative. Yet, it was always crafted to communicate eternal truths. Knowing a bit of background helps understand the land as the *Fifth Gospel*.

WHOSE IMAGE

A group of Pharisees and Herodians, hero worshipers of

Herod, seeking to impale Jesus on the horns of a dilemma, asked Him a question to which, it seemed to them, there was no answer with which He could win. They asked if it was right to pay taxes to Caesar.

If He said yes, He would incur the wrath of the Jews for implying Caesar was head over Israel and not God. If He said the tax should not be paid, He would make Himself an enemy of Rome. It appeared He was trapped.

Instead, Jesus asked for a coin and, holding it up, asked, "Whose image and inscription is this?" Their answer, "Caesar's." His response, "Render therefore unto Caesar the things that are Caesar's and to God the thing that are God's" (Matthew 22: 15 - 23). In other words, Jesus' instructions said to give Caesar the coin bearing his image and give God your heart, mind, soul, and body which bear His image.

EVERY GOOD AND EVERY PERFECT GIFT

Few passages of Scripture contain more distinctly figurative language than James 1: 17: "Every good gift and every perfect gift is from above, and comes down from the Father of Lights, with whom there is no variation or show of turning." It is both literally true and graphically illustrative. In the text there are two different nouns, both of which are translated *gift*:

- The first, *dosos,* means the act of giving.
- The second, *dorema,* means, *the thing*, the actual gift.

Hence, "Every good giving and every perfect gift is from above." These gifts come from the *The Father of Lights,* depicting God as Creator. The sun, moon, and stars declare Him. Genesis 1: 16 says, "He made the greater light, the sun, the lesser light, the moon, and the stars."

Albert Einstein once asked his students at Humboldt University in Berlin how much knowledge collectively they considered themselves to have. They gave the enormous estimate of five percent. In response he answered, "Is it possible God exists in the 95 percent you don't know?" The simple fact of God's creation is even more amazing when anyone considers the greatness of God's universe. A typical galaxy contains billions of individual stars: Earth's galaxy alone, the Milky Way, contains two hundred billion stars. The average distance between one galaxy and another is about twenty million trillion miles. The closest galaxy is the Andromeda Galaxy, about twelve million trillion miles away.

For every effect, there must be a cause. This is a basic law of physics. The universe is an *effect*. An effect is the result of a *cause*. There can be no effect without a cause. To be more specific, for there to be the effect, which is the universe, there must be an *equal* or *greater* cause. God is the greater Cause.

God is depicted as a God "with whom there is no variableness." *Variableness* translates the Greek word *parallage*, a word that refers to change or variation. Our English equivalent is the word *parallax*. It carries the meaning of changing a point of view. God is constant and consistent.

He is the God with whom there is no "shadow of turning." This depicts the lengthening late afternoon shadows creeping across the landscape to the east. The turning of the earth casts the shadows. The sun remains constant; it doesn't turn away. God, like the sun, doesn't turn away. He is constant.

As the light of the sun is constant, so is God. As the sun doesn't change, neither does God. At night the sun hasn't stopped shining. The earth has simply turned. He is like the sun, we like the earth. If people experience spiritual darkness, it is not because God has changed; it is because they have turned away from Him.

STILL WATER

The Psalmist spoke of "still water" and God like a good shepherd leading His people to it (Psalm 23).

In the Bible Land, it rains only a few months a year. The rest of the year, the land is dry and devoid of water. The good shepherd, knowing this, prepares for the drought.

Finding a cave, a socket in the ground, he lines it with plaster, making it a cistern. He then gathers stone on the hillside making a large V with the tip of the V being at the mouth of the cistern. When it rains, the water is funneled into the cistern. When water is not exposed to light or air, it remains fresh almost indefinitely. Thus, the shepherd has stored up the water the sheep need long before it is needed. This is called "still water."

Our Heavenly Father has in store for us what we need long before we need it.

MY GOD, MY GOD

Of Jesus' seven cries from the cross, the one most shrouded in mystery is, "My God, my God, why have you forsaken me?" At the time, the Old Testament was not divided into chapters and verses. When a child was taught a Scripture, the parent would quote the opening line of the passage to identify it. In this way the child would know what passage was to be recited. These first words of a passage were known as *incipits*, meaning *it begins*. Jesus' cry identified Psalm 22, which opens with these words. In effect, He was saying, "If you want to know what is happening here, look it up in Psalm 22."

PETER: I GO FISHING

After receiving the news of the Resurrection, Simon Peter exclaimed, "I am going fishing." Indications are Peter was a successful professional fisherman. One of the most popular items in the fish markets of Rome was salted fish from the Galilee. He could have become quite successful as a fisherman.

His assertion of going fishing is understood by some to mean he was disheartened, giving up, and going back to his old trade.

His statement needs to be understood in light of what the angel told the women at the tomb on Jesus' resurrection morning:

"Go and tell His disciples—and Peter—that He is going before you into Galilee; and there you will see Him..." (Mark 16: 7).

In light of this good news, it is likely that what Peter meant by "I am going fishing" is "I am going where Jesus said He would be." It was his excited way of believing and wanting to see his risen Lord.

FISHERMEN OF MEN OR SHEPHERDS

Jesus used two distinct terms regarding the ministry of His followers. In calling His disciples, He called them to be "fishers of men." After His resurrection, He instructed them to feed and shepherd His sheep. The first metaphor refers to evangelism, reaching those without faith. The second relates to pastoral ministry, caring for the flock. It is not an *either/or*, but a *both/and*.

The best times to fish in the Galilee were winter and spring. In the rainy season, the Jordan River gets swollen and brings to the sea much organic matter through the spring. During these seasons, the fish come up closer to the surface to feed because the sun warms the surface water. The water in certain areas of the sea is warmed by hot springs feeding into it along certain shorelines of the sea. In the summer, the fish go into deeper parts of the sea to avoid the heat. During this time, they do not feed as often.

Sheep demonstrate their greatest need for the care of a shepherd at the very time fishing is poorest. Many individuals were both fishermen and shepherds.

In a spiritual sense, followers of Jesus can do both, evangelize and provide pastoral care.

MOUNTAIN MOVERS

Jesus said, "If you have faith as a mustard seed, you shall say to this mountain, 'Remove hence to yonder place and it shall remove...'" (Matthew 17: 20).

It is commonly believed He was looking at and referring to the

Herodian, a mountain made by Herod the Great. Perhaps He was; however, there was a metaphor common in the era that was perhaps His reference.

A problem was referred to as a *mountain*. Persons with the ability to resolve issues and solve problems were called mountain movers. Applying that understanding, the expression can be seen as faith, enabling persons to deal with and solve problems. Thus, it is an encouragement to faith.

COVENANT OF SALT

Jesus said, "Salt is good, but if the salt loses its flavor, how will you season it? Have salt in yourselves and have peace with one another" (Mark 9: 50).

This statement was made against the Old Testament instruction for all offerings to be accompanied by salt: "With all your offerings you shall offer salt" (Leviticus 2: 13).

Salt was a very essential, rare, and valuable product. The word for it is the word from which comes the English word *salary*. It was so highly regarded that it was considered a commodity of value in business.

When people ate together, they became friends often exchanging the expression, "There is salt between us." It spoke of hospitality and friendship. Covenants were often confirmed by a sacrificial meal with salt always present.

Salt, being a preservative, became a symbol of enduring friendship and commitment. The Lord spoke to Aaron of "a covenant of salt forever... "(Numbers 18:19).

God gave the dominion over Israel to David "by a covenant of salt..." (II Chronicles 13: 5). Therefore, in speaking of salt losing its flavor, Jesus is referring to a covenant, that is, a promise, not being kept and losing its worth, not providing its benefit.

Every covenant involves a condition and a consequence, a

requirement and a result. To not keep the condition or requirement is to forfeit the consequence or result. The analogy is that when a commitment is made and broken, the salt has lost its flavor; it is useless.

BREAD AND SALT

Names of places have meaning in the Orient. The name Bethlehem means *house of bread* in Hebrew and Aramaic. In ancient Near East cultures, bread was considered a basic ingredient of human life.

Since Neolithic times, wheat, the basis of bread, has been associated with the life cycle. Jesus used it when He referred to his pending death in saying, "Unless a grain of wheat falls to the ground and dies, it remains alone; but if it dies, it produces much grain" (John 12: 24).

Jesus said of Himself, "I am the bread of life; he who comes to me shall never hunger" (John 6: 35).

Bread is treated with great respect in the Near East. It is often blessed when the dough is being kneaded with the words, "In the name of God." Mistreatment of bread was considered great disrespect. If a piece of bread were found on the ground, it was picked up, blessed, and put in a safe, clean place. Even today in some remote villages, old bread is put in plastic bags and hung outside the trash bin.

A term of endearment is "Between us there is bread symbolizing life and salt." If an individual is being inducted into an order upon being approved, it is said, "Do not betray the rights of salt and bread." The symbolic significance of salt runs deep in the Old Testament. The covenant between God and the Jews was a salt covenant.

Among those who know the significance, the sharing of bread and salt is an ancestral basis of hospitality, a right of friendship which cancels any estrangement and creates an indissoluble mutual obligation of protection.

A believer's faith in Jesus Christ is based on Him as the Bread of Life. A commitment to Him carries the import of a bread and salt commitment.

Today in Nazareth, there is a restaurant with a sign out front reading, "We have a salt room." It is a place where agreements and commitments are made. Every church should be such.

MILK AND HONEY

There were three types of honey; one is produced by bees and the other two are fruit nectar, date and fig honey. In the Holy Land, date trees grow most places, but they only produce abundantly in fertile soil with adequate water. For them to flow with honey, they must be well nourished.

Bee honey was a part of the Jewish culture and diet. An apiary consisting of thirty clay cylindrical beehives has been found at Tel Rehov in the northeast Jordan Valley dating to three thousand years ago. This indicates beekeeping for the valued honey and wax has long been practiced in the country. The presence of bees indicated flowering plants in the area which necessitate soil supportive of plant growth, meaning the land was fertile.

The Talmud interprets the expression as "milk flows from the goats' [utter], and honey flows from figs" (Ketu'bot 111b).

These two figures were extremely appealing to the Hebrews coming out of the barren desert. Used together, they speak of the abundance of the land.

Though the two are real, the term serves as a metaphor for a good, fertile land that produces profusely.

LOCUST AND HONEY

John the Baptist ate locust and wild honey. *Locust* here is not to be confused with the insect locust. In fact, locusts as insects did not thrive in the barren desert area in which John ministered, but the locust tree which bears fruit does predominate in the desert region. Locust fruit was a carob-like bean produced by the *Ceratonia siliequa*, commonly known as the carob tree, sometimes referred to as St. John's bread. It is in the bean family, *Fabaceae*. The pods are flat, curved, and brown with a purplish tint and contain a sticky-pulp and bean like seed. The pulp tastes like chocolate and is used in baking and syrup and is dried for later use. In the form of St. John's bread, it is available in specialty bakeries.

Bees, on the other hand, refer to just bees and their product, honey. Bees in the Holy Land make their honey in the crevices of rocks and trees. It is especially nutritious. In addition to being a nourishing food, it has many medicinal uses and was a very good preservative of other foods. Hence, the diet of John the Baptist was basically bread and honey. Combined, the two formed the basis of a primitive survival diet.

WINE

Ancients had several ways of preserving unfermented wine. One way was to reduce the grape juice to the constituency of a thick syrup or even jelly known in Hebrew as *debhash* and in Arabic *dbs*. This preserved form could be used over a long period of time. With water added, the concentrate turned the water to unfermented wine.

Sometimes a cake was made of dried grapes which later had water added to produce unfermented wine.

"Do not look on the wine when it is red, when it sparkles in the cup, when it swirls around smoothly; at last it bites like a serpent, and stings like a viper" (Proverbs 23: 31,32).

Movement in wine is caused by bubbles resulting from fermentation. The Greeks, seeing movement in the wine, thought it indicated there was life in the wine. When wine was consumed, it influenced speech, hearing, and ambulation. Because of this outside control of the body, they thought it to be a god and gave the god the name *Baccah*.

When the Bible appeals for persons not to be filled with wine but be "filled with the Spirit" (Ephesians 5:18), it is teaching persons to choose the true God, the Holy Spirit, not Baccah. It means to let the Holy Spirit control the body.

Wine was in common use in the Bible time. It is helpful to understand how it was used in deciding how to apply Bible verses related to it.

Wine was normally stored in large, pointed jugs called *amphorae*. When it was to be used, the desired portion was poured from the amphorae into large bowls known as *kraters*. From the kraters, the cups, known as *kylixes*, were filled. In the large bowl, the kraters, water was added before the mixture was used to fill the cups.

The ratio of water to wine varied. Different ancient writers note different formulas ranging from one part of wine to twenty parts of water. Others indicate a ratio of one to five, one to four, or two to five.

At the wedding of Cana, Jesus had the water, pots filled with water and when the guests drank, they referred to it as *wine*, the normal word for the mixture of water and wine.

Writers normally referred to wine mixed with water as wine. Wine not mixed with water it was called unmixed *(akratesteron)* wine.

Drinking wine without its being mixed with water was looked upon as Scythian or barbarian.

Plutarch wrote, "We call a mixture 'wine,' although the larger of the component parts is water."

The Jewish Encyclopedia states that during the Rabbinic period *yayin* (wine) was to be distinguished from *shekar* (strong drink): the former is diluted with water (*mazug*); the latter is undiluted (*yayin hai*).

The Persahim 108b portion of the Talmud states that for the four cups every Jew was to drink from during the Passover ritual, the mix was a ratio of three parts water to one part of wine. From this can be concluded that what Jesus and the disciples used at the Last Supper was not an intoxicant.

Clement of Alexandria stated, "It is best for the wine to be mixed with as much water as possible.... For both are works of God, and the mixing of the two, both the water and wine, produces health...."

The mixture of water and wine was also used for medicinal purposes. Because of amoeba in water, wine was added as a purifying agent. Hence, the Scripture says, "Drink no longer water, but use a little wine for the stomach's sake and thine often infirmities" (I Timothy 5:23). Wine was a disinfectant also.

ANOINTING WITH OIL

Believers are urged to engage in anointing with oil and prayer (James 5: 14, 15).

In the Greek text there are two words for *anoint*.

Chris is one. It is the root for the Greek name *Christos,* the English name for Christ. *Christos* means The Anointed One. In the Old Testament era, prophets, priests, and kings were anointed by putting olive oil on their foreheads. Christ is our Prophet, Priest, and King.

Alepho is the other word used in James. It meant to massage or knead into the body. The material used was either olive oil or another ointment. Both had some of the best medicinal properties of the time. Therefore, if followers are going to do literally what the passage actually says, they should not put oil on the brow, but massage the body with olive oil.

What the text teaches is the use of the best medicine available. Such oil and ointments were among the best medicine of the time of the writing by James. Jewish Rabbis writing at the same time recorded their confidence in such treatment. In the story of the Good Samaritan, the man who had been beaten was anointed with oil. It had a healing effect and stopped bleeding.

Based on what is actually taught in James, it is not proper simply to put oil on the brow of a sick person and pray. The appeal made by James is for the best medicine available to be used along with prayer. Therefore, it is expedient that proper medical treatment be used. This is a commendation of the use of medicine.

Likewise, the urgent appeal in James is for prayer for the sick. Faithful Christians should privately and collectively pray.

Once these two things have been done, then all that God requires has been done. God's response is then based on His love and knowledge. Confidently, persons having done what the Lord asks can be assured that whether their beloved is healed or not, they did all God required by using the best medicine available and praying.

Medicinal oils available for various healing purposes were these:

- Aloe, a stimulant and cardiac tonic, digestive benefits
- Cedarwood, antioxidant essential healing oil
- Cypress, antibacterial
- Frankincense, antimicrobial and immune stimulant
- Galbanum, antimicrobial, to be taken orally
- Hyssop, antifungal, antibacterial, larvicidal
- Myrtle, antimicrobial and antioxidant
- Onycha, antioxidant
- Myrrh plus frankincense, a synergetic healing effect imposing antimicrobial benefits

Some of these were occasionally mixed with olive oil and various unguents, which also had healing properties.

THE LAST SUPPER

Jesus gathered with His disciples on the eve of His execution to celebrate the Passover. The Passover is based on Exodus 20, wherein God instructed the Israelites in Egypt to sacrifice a lamb at twilight on the fourteenth day of the Jewish month of Nisan, before sunset, and eat it after sundown. According to Jewish tradition, a new day began with sunset. Thus, they sacrificed the lamb on the fourteenth day and ate it on the fifteenth. Originally, that was the evening before the massive exodus from slavery in Egypt.

As recorded in John 13, the text makes it apparent that the Roman style of dining was practiced. The host and guests would have reclined around a center table propped up on their left elbows. Customarily, there was a hierarchy with guests placed in accordance with their standing with the group. As they reclined, each person's head was nearest the table and the body reclined at an angle away from the table. The angle of the recline was such that a person faced the table at a slight angle. The head of each diner was near the chest of the one behind him. The historian Pliny noted one diner was said to lie "in the bosom" of another. The person to the left of the principal person was slightly behind that person. This was the position of honor. The one to the right of the principal person was in the second place of honor.

The order in which they reclined enabled the disciple "whom Jesus loved" to lean on Jesus' chest (John13: 23). This was a title given John. Being in this position would indicate his prominence among the disciples.

Jesus indicated one disciple would betray Him. Peter asked John who it was. John leaned back on Jesus' chest and asked, "Lord, who is it?" John would have been close enough that this could have been private inquiry not heard by all. Jesus said it would be the one to whom He would give a dipped piece of bread. He gave it to Judas who was close enough to receive it. That means Judas was immediately to Jesus' left, the place of honor.

The sequence of inquiries and events indicates that perhaps only John and Peter knew what it meant when Jesus gave the bread to Judas. Being given such a morsel by the principal person was a traditional mark of esteem and regard. The other disciples, seeing Jesus give the bread to Judas likely perceived of it in that light, not as an indication of the recipient being the betrayer.

Earlier in the evening, Jesus had washed the feet of Judas, as

He had all of the disciples. Thus, Jesus was showing sacrificial love and service to His enemy. The giving of the dipped bread was a last opportunity offered Judas to change. By accepting the bread, knowing it identified him as the betrayer, Judas showed himself unmoved by the loving overtures shown him by Jesus.

ON THE RIGHT HAND

Jesus is represented as being on the Father's right hand. Commentators often associate this power with authority. In the biblical era some courts had the chief magistrate sit on an elevated platform. Two judges sat, one on his left and one on his right. When the magistrate made a decision regarding the one charged, he either turned to the judge on his left and ordered him to write a bill of condemnation or to the judge on his right and instructed him to write a bill of acquittal.

Jesus' depiction as being on the Father's right is postured as the one who writes a bill of acquittal, depending on the judgment of the court of Heaven based upon the faith of the person.

JESUS' PRESENCE

One of the few times that Jesus is quoted in the New Testament outside the four gospels, He is recorded as saying, "I will never leave you nor forsake you" (Hebrews 13: 5).

In that statement are five compound synergistic negatives: "I will never, no not ever, no never leave you behind, abandon you, give up on you, or send you back."

That is a forever *never* with no exceptions ever.

What is said is important. Who says it is as important as the statement itself. It is vital to consider the source. Jesus, Immanuel, God with us made that statement. We must observe, "He Himself" said it. Who is He?

He is all-powerful. To use the theological term, He is

omnipotent. He who spoke the universe into existence has the power to do what He says He will do.

He is all-present. Again, the theological term is *omnipresent*, meaning, all present. He who was present when the first flower bloomed in Eden made that statement. He is the Alpha and Omega, the center and circumference of life, the apogee and the perigee of our existence. He it is Who is present to perform.

He is all knowing. Once again, a theological term *omniscient* is used, meaning He is all knowing. "I will never, no not ever, no never abandon you, give up on you, send you back, cause you not to survive, or leave you helpless." He has the knowledge to know what to do.

When feeling without strength to carry on, Christians should remember that it is the omnipotent, the all-powerful God who said, "I will never, no not ever, no never abandon you, give up on you, send you back, cause you not to survive, or leave you helpless."

When feeling all alone, remember it is the omnipresent, all present God who said, "I will never, no not ever, no never abandon you, give up on you, send you back, cause you not to survive, or leave you helpless." He is present with you.

When not knowing what to do, remember it is the omniscient, the all-knowing God who said, "I will never, no not ever, no never abandon you, give up on you, send you back, cause you not to survive, or leave you helpless." He will illumine your understanding.

Jesus wants His followers to practice the Presence behind the promise, realizing He will never, no not ever, no never leave you.

TRUTHFUL BUT NOT ACTUAL

Often a literal truth misses the intended fact. In speaking of avoiding adultery, Jesus said, "And if your right eye causes you to sin, pluck it out and cast it from you; for it is more profitable for you that one of your members perish, than for your whole body to be cast into hell. And if your right hand causes you to sin, cut it off and cast it from you; for it is more profitable that one of your members perish, than for your whole body to be cast into hell" (Matthew 5: 29-30).

It is not Jesus' desire that this should be done literally. Doing so seems extreme, but it does not go far enough in avoiding sin. One could carry out the acts literally and still sin. The eye and hand are not the cause of sin, but the consequences. Jesus identifies the matrix of sin saying, "For out of the heart proceed evil thoughts, murders, adulteries, fornications, thefts, false witness, blasphemies" (Matthew 15:19).

The Greek word *kardia*, translated heart, does not simply refer to the center for the circulation of the blood. It is a reference to the center and seat of spiritual life. It was used of the foundation of intelligence, passion, desire, appetites, character, and will.

In the biblical era, there was one school of thought that believed ideas originated in the heart and were carried by the blood to the brain where they became conscious thoughts.

It is there, the heart, the control center of life; avoidance of the inclination to sin is to be enacted. The plucking out of the eye and cutting off of the hand, though not literal, are an indication of how serious the act of avoidance is.

Persons who have flashes of evil thoughts often feel guilty for having such thoughts. Such thoughts are not sin unless the person gives tangible consent to them. Dismissing them is an act of not yielding to temptation. It is sage wisdom that reveals "you can't keep the birds from flying over your head, but you can keep them from nesting in your hair."

Doing so is a positive response to the admonition to "flee also youthful lusts; but pursue righteousness, faith, love, peace with those who call on the Lord out of a pure heart" (II Timothy 2: 2).

HATE FATHER AND MOTHER

Jesus said, "If anyone comes to Me and does not hate his father and mother, wife and children, brothers and sisters, yes, and his own life also, he cannot be My disciple" (Luke 14: 26).

This is an example of Jesus using comparative language. It is not a literal appeal to hate one's own, but compared to one's love for Him, an individual's love, even strong love, for others is as though it were hate. Being a true follower of Jesus makes one love family and others.

THE LAW

In Scripture there are three classifications of law:

- **The Ceremonial Law**, or *hakkim*, means custom of the nation. It formed the basis for worship by Israel during the era of the Bible. The law was designed to direct the people toward the coming Messiah. Christ's coming fulfilled these laws, and they, being fulfilled, are no longer applicable. The beginning of the New Covenant brought to an end over six hundred Old Testament Ceremonial Laws.
- **Old Testament Civil Laws** (Judicial Laws) were designed to give guidance in daily interpersonal living only in the Old Testament era. With the dissolution of ancient Israel, they became passé.
- **The Moral Law**, or *mishpatim*, reveals the nature and will of God and is still universally applicable. By them God's holiness and man's unholiness are revealed. The Ten Commandments are an example of the Moral Law. They are not an intended means of obtaining saving grace.

THIS DAY THE LORD HAS MADE

Prophetically, the Old Testament often focuses light on New Testament reality. "This is the day the Lord has made; we will rejoice and be glad in it" (Psalm 118: 24) is such a passage.

Moderns often quote this verse as a reference to a twenty-four-hour day. Though it is relevant to the present day, it actually spoke of a prophetic day, the day Messiah would come. The early Christians were rejoicing because of that coming day. Currently, there is reason to apply the verse to the future day of Jesus' Second Coming and also reason to rejoice every day because of the day He came and will come again.

THE CHURCH

The first Christians were Jews. Even some Pharisees became Christians. Initially, they did not envision themselves as having forsaken Judaism. An initial question was whether non-Jews have to become Jews before they could become Christians (Acts 15)? The early Christians continued to observe the Sabbath, but also the Lord's Day, on Sundays.

The real Jesus Movement was launched on the Day of Pentecost following the resurrection of Jesus Christ (Acts 2). The Book of Acts chronicles the expeditious growth of the faith. Persons from seventeen countries were numbered among the three thousand who responded to Peter's message delivered on the steps into the Temple Mount after the Resurrection. They were baptized in the mikvas along the steps (Acts 2: 41). Later, in response to hearing of the Resurrection, there were five thousand respondents in faith (Acts 4: 4). Not long after, it is reported that on Solomon's Porch, "Believers were increasingly added to the Lord, multitudes of men and women" (Acts 5: 14).

Acts record that as the Apostles shared the good news, it was said of them, "You have filled Jerusalem with your doctrine" (Acts 5: 28). "Daily in the temple, and in every house, they did not cease teaching and preaching Jesus as the Christ"(Acts 5: 42).

Persecution of Christians increased. In 70, the sixty-thousand-member Roman army under Vespasian laid siege to and destroyed Jerusalem and the Temple. Most Jews were killed, committed suicide, or fled. This ended the Levitical priesthood and sacrificial system. The Jewish religion was silenced. This resulted in the Christian community being virtually disassociated with Judaism.

The Apostles were dispersed and carried the gospel to other regions. Throughout the islands and coastal regions around the Mediterranean, the gospel was spread by Jewish Christian slaves on ships. Members of the numerous Jewish communities scattered through the vast area received the Word from the slaves who reported the Crucifixion and Resurrection.

The evolution of the name for the place where Christians assembled was gradual. For some time, Gentiles who became Christians as well as Judeo-Christians called their places of worship synagogues. In Hebrew, houses of worship were called *Bet Knesset*, meaning House of Assembly. As the Hellenistic influence grew, this became *synagogue*, which in Greek means assembly.

The Jewish community used its synagogues for numerous purposes such as study of Scripture, Shabbat and feast-day sermons, collection and depository of community funds, and religious tribunals.

At Benais, Jesus foretold this expansion would happen when He said, "I will build my church."

Skeptics have been critical of this statement by Jesus (Matthew 16: 18), noting that at the time of the statement there was no church. Such a conclusion is based on the Western concept of church as an institution and/or building.

The word that Jesus judiciously chose for church is *ekklesia*, meaning a called-out assembly. It was a secular Greek word with no religious connotation.

To distinguish themselves from the Jewish community, the Christians began to use the Greek word *ekklesia*, employed by Jesus. It soon was applied to the place of meeting as well as to those meeting there.

Later, another Greek word came into use regarding the body: *kyriake,* meaning belonging to the Lord (*kyrios*). From this came the English word church. Technically, the word *church* means belonging to the Lord.

Jesus had begun His building process.

THE JESUS OF THE BIBLE

Having given consideration to the land, the language, and the lore, it is appropriate to give thought to the One who motivates interest in the subject, the One who in the Bible is called Lord, Jesus Christ. Who was this One?

The Gospel of John opens, "In the beginning..." (John1:1). Literally translated, the text means before time began to begin. Time, matter, and space were the three primary parts of creation.

Before time began to begin "was the Word." This translates the Greek *Logos*. To understand the meaning of a word, one must observe how it was used at the time of its use.

Writing about the same time as John, Philo, the Jewish Hellenistic philosopher, used *Word* to mean all that is known or knowable about God.

Earlier Heraclitus, a pre-Socratic Greek philosopher, used it to mean the ordering principle for the universe.

Combining these two uses of *Logos* in the Book of John means all that is known or knowable about God, the ordering principle for the universe. That One is Jesus.

John follows this introduction with a further revelation: "The Word (Logos) was with God, and the Word was God."

This poses the question of how He could be God and be with God.

He was God in essence: that is, He was the very essential essence of God. He was not just like God, He was God.

Positionally, He was with God the Father. This introduces the concept of the Trinity, three in one.

The Trinity and the divine nature of Jesus Christ are adroitly described in I Timothy 3:16: "Great is the mystery of godliness...."

The curtain call for the Trinity is Genesis 1: 26: "In the beginning God (*Elohim*, plural) said, 'Let us make man in our own image.'" The plural name for God speaks of the Trinity.

The Shema, Deuteronomy 6: 4-5, states, "Hear, O Israel: The Lord our God, the Lord is one!" (KJV).

"Hear, O Israel: The LORD our God, the LORD is one" (NIV).

Herein two names are used for *Lord* and *God*. It reads, "The Jehovah (singular) our Elohim, (plural) is one (singular) Jehovah."

A key to understanding is the word *ech*, translated One. *Ech* is not the word for a digit, but a unit. Illustrative of this, one (unit) pack of gum consists of five pieces. Or, one (unit) carton of Cokes is comprised of six Cokes. One (unit) God consists of three as one.

When John the Baptist was baptizing in the Jordan, the Trinity made a cameo appearance. Jesus, God the Son, came to be baptized; God, the Holy Spirit in the likeness of a dove, came down; and the voice of God, the Father, was heard to say, "This is my beloved Son, in whom I am well pleased" (Matthew 3:17).

An understanding of the Trinity is further illustrated in math. $1+1+1=3$; however, $1 \times 1 \times 1=1$.

The chemical composition H_2O as a liquid is water, in a solid state it is ice, and as steam it is a vapor. In neither state does its nature change. H_2O is three in one.

Jesus Christ, God the Son, is spoken of in Romans 9: 5: "Christ came, who is over all, the eternally blessed God."

Colossians 1: 19, speaking of Jesus, states: "For it pleased the Father that in Him all the fullness should dwell."

Fullness translates *plurama*, meaning the absolute completeness. The reference is to Jesus being in totality God.

Philippians 2: 5 - 8 further emphasizes Jesus' dual nature as the God/man-man/God: "Christ Jesus, who, being in the form of God, did not consider it robbery to be equal to God, but made Himself of no reputation, taking the form of a servant, and coming in the likeness of men." The word *form* (vs. 6) translates the Greek word *morphe*, (Vs. 7) and relates to His essence, His nature. That being God. In verse 7 the Greek word *homoioma*, referring to His external appearance, is translated likeness of men.

In verse 8, the Greek word *schema* is translated fashion or in some translations, appearance, making further reference to His external form. Externally, He became a man while internally remaining God. Play-Doh shaped as a sphere is still Play-Doh. Shaped as a cube, its form has changed, but its nature has not. Jesus' external form changed, but inwardly He was still God.

As an aid in further understanding the nature of Jesus Christ, the term *Son of God* is employed.

When Jesus Christ stepped across the threshold of Heaven and over the rampart of earth, He came as Mary's cooing child, the *Son of God*. As the prophet Isaiah had long before promised, "Unto us a child was born," Mary's baby; "Unto us a son is given" (Isaiah 9: 6), God's Son. In Scripture Jesus Christ is repetitiously called the Son of God:

- Jesus Himself declared, "I said, I am the Son of God" (John 10:36).
- Gabriel told Mary her child would be called "the Son of God" (Luke 1: 32, 33).
- Satan identified Him as "the Son of God" at the time of His temptations (Matt. 4: 3. 7).
- John the Baptist spoke of Him at His baptism as "the Son of God" (John 1: 34).
- The Centurion at the cross said surely this was "the Son of God" (Matt. 27: 54).

The term *son* is not used in the sense of prodigy, offspring. It speaks of association, not generation. The dictionary, as well as Scripture, recognizes the title as referring to association, not generation.

James and John were called "Sons of Thunder." The name Barnabas means "Son of Encouragement."

Today, individuals are often called sons or daughters of America.

Scripture does not call Jesus a Son, but the Son of God.

Human beings are also called "sons of God." A different term is used in referring to Jesus as the Son of God and a human being referred to as a son of God.

The Greek word *teknon* is used in reference to humans. It stresses the fact of birth. We are born again as a *teknon*. The Greek word *huios* is used of Jesus. It emphasizes dignity and character of relationship. Thus, it identifies Jesus as deity.

In Jesus the *pleroma*, fullness, permanently dwells. The fullness of the Godhead, *theotetos*, divinity, dwells in Jesus. *Theotetos* means not just divine attributes, but the very essence, the nature of God, the totality of Who God the Father is, His supreme nature. Concisely, Jesus is Immanuel, God with us, God incarnate (in flesh). His eternal pre-creation God nature was manifested bodily.

Second Corinthians 4:4 records: "Christ, who is the image of God...." *Ekkon* means He is the perfect, visible likeness of the invisible God in both personality and distinctive attributes. He is Immanuel, God with us.

The Son, Jesus, is said to have been "born of a woman" (Galatians 4: 4) meaning born without human paternity, born only of a woman, a virgin.

Summarily, it is said of Jesus:

Without controversy great is the mystery of godliness:
God was manifested in the flesh,
Justified in the Spirit,
Seen by angels,
Preached among the Gentiles,
Believed on in the world,
Received up in glory.

~ I Timothy 3: 16

HOW TO GET THE MOST OUT OF A VISIT TO THE BIBLE LAND

Tourists, learners, Bible students—all visitors blessed enough to find themselves in the Holy Land—will receive the greatest benefit from time spent in this hallowed ground if they will free the spirit and follow these points of advice which travelers or natives of the region would share:

- Live the moment! In visiting the Bible Land, be there. Commit your loved ones and life back home to the Lord and free your mind for a new adventure.
- Live in the present. Don't give in to flashbacks of *this reminds me of*. Enjoy what is.
- Don't let trivial happenings around you distract you from the significance of where you are.
- Historically, the land has many layers. Don't let the present preoccupy you and keep you from enjoying reflecting on the historical significance of the past, particularly the Bible time.
- Don't be distracted by constantly asking, "Is this the actual place?" The tour guide will most often verify if it is or use such expressions as *traditionally*, *commemorates*, or *allegedly* to let you know if a place is authentic. It is often difficult to know for sure. Enjoy the historical event associated with each place, not just the place.
- Savor the setting and don't expect exactness in every instance.
- Don't hide behind your camera so much that you fail to soak in your surroundings visually.
- Brush off rude individuals and awkward circumstances. Don't let them diminish your spirit.
- Remember you have come on a pilgrimage, and your schedule might fatigue you. Stay as fresh as possible, but don't complain about conditions and schedule.
- Enjoy the food and beverages of the land. You can get that good cup of coffee when you get home, but you can't get the native brew at home. Enjoy the difference.

Most pilgrims want to walk where Jesus walked. It is impossible to say with certainty exactly where He walked. There are a few places where it is logical that He did walk. He is said to have visited the synagogues in the Galilee. Any synagogue in the area from His era was likely visited by Him. The Herodian Street at the southwest corner of the Temple Mount was a busy thoroughfare He likely traveled. The steps leading up to the Double and Triple Doors of the Temple Mount at the southern side of the Temple Mount are a location where He walked. It is a good place for pilgrims to take off their shoes and take a photo of their feet standing on the street—standing where the great I AM stood. Ultimately, no doubt, the most important admonition about a visit to the Holy Land is to open the heart and mind to the Essence, the Light, to God Himself for the profoundest of experiences.

EPILOGUE

A pilgrimage through the Bible Land, whether through touching the soil or gazing at the ancient stones, is certain to transform the individual life. A realization of a perfect creation shattered by evil seizes the mind. The reality that events there changed the world and are changing the world and will change the world permeates the air. Then, a solacing gratitude surges in the stale soul for the redemption—the salvation for a fallen Earth—that took place in this land of Hallowed Light. Ultimately, an overwhelming current of Love and Good elevates the spirit to become a "new man"—a renewed person, a wiser person, a healed person.

This is the power *of the Land*, the power *of the message of the land*, but—most overwhelming—the power *of the Person* Who lived as a pauper *in* the land and Who will return as the King *to* the land. It was to this nation that the Hallowed Light—Jesus, God Himself—came to accept the greatest burden of history, *and* it is the place to which the Living Light will one day come again to declare the greatest victory. This is the Land of the Bible.

Israel is God's chosen land. His Holy Ground. The land on which the Hallowed Light shines. This is, indeed, a land which carries with it the declaration of blessings and curses. God, once again, trumpets the Truth from the pages of His Word. To respect the land, to revere the events, and to embrace the Person of the land is to choose life over death as declared in the sobering words of God Himself:

I will bless those who bless you,

And I will curse him who curses you; and in you all the families of the earth shall be blessed.

~Genesis 12:3

GLOSSARY

Al-Aqsa Mosque – A mosque originally built on the site in 705. The present silver-domed Al-Aqsa mosque was built in 1035. It is considered the third most holy place in the Muslim world. The area is known among Muslims as the Noble Sanctuary and by the Jews as the Temple Mount. It is a mosque and not to be confused with the gold-domed Dome of the Rock which is a shrine, not a mosque.

Aretas IV – Nabataean ruler between 9 BC and 40 whose jurisdiction extended from Petra to Damascus. For a time, he was the father-in-law of Herod Antipas. In Damascus Paul escaped the search for him by King Aretas IV by being lowered down the city wall in a basket (II Corinthians 11: 32, 33).

Canaanites – Named for Canaan, a grandson of Noah, people who dwelt in the land of Canaan, an area including parts of modern-day Israel, Palestine, Lebanon, Syria, and Jordan.

City of David – The original city built by David who lived around 1000 BC. It is a short distance south of the present Dung Gate, occupying a ridge formed by the convergence of the Kidron Valley on the east and the Central Valley on the west. It was protected on the north by the palace and fortress and shielded on the other sides by the valleys. It was constructed on the site of the Jebusite City and conquered by David in the eighteenth-century BC (II Samuel 5: 6, 7).

Diaspora – Refers to the exiling or scattering of Israelites, Judahites, and later Jews out of their ancestral homeland, Israel. The diaspora started with the exile to Babylon. The Jewish state came to an end in 70 with the conquest by the Romans who scattered them.

Dome of the Rock – An Islamic shrine, not a mosque, built by Umayy Abd al-Malik ibn Marwan on the site formerly occupied by the Roman temple of Jupiter and before that by the Second Temple of the Jews. An inscription in the building notes the date of completion as 691-692. It is believed to be built over the site where Abraham expressed a willingness to sacrifice Isaac and the locale from which Muhammad is said to have ascended into Heaven. The gold dome is made of gilt aluminum and bronze overlaid with 80 kilograms of gold worth over $1.4 million. It is not to be confused with the silver-domed Al-Aqsa Mosque also located on the Temple Mount.

Druze – A distinct minority among Arabs in modern Israel. Their faith developed out of Islam, but they do not consider themselves Muslims. Their faith is based on covert oral traditions.

Ecce Homo Arch – *Behold the man*, the words spoken by Pilate regarding Jesus. The freestanding arch was built by Hadrian in 135 AD to commemorate his victory over the Jews.

Edicule – The *Edicule*, from the Latin a*edicule* meaning little house. A small structure within the Church of the Holy Sepulcher encloses the remains of a cave that has been venerated since the last of the fourth century as the tomb of Jesus Christ. Entrance into the tomb portion is through an eleven by thirteen-foot anti-chamber known as the Chapel of the Angels, which commemorates where the angel made the announcement of the Resurrection. When representatives of Constantine arrived in Jerusalem in 325, there was a Roman temple dedicated to Venus on the site. Buildings dedicated to other deities than Jesus were often built over sites venerated by Christians to defame them. The top part of the cave in which Jesus is believed to have been buried was shaved off to expose the burial site, and an edicule was built on the location. It was destroyed in 1009 and later rebuilt.

Essenes – Pious separatist Jews who dwelt in Khirbet Qumran on the west bank of the Dead Sea. The Dead Sea Scrolls found in the area are normally associated with them.

Hasidic Judaism – A branch of Orthodox Judaism that promotes spirituality by popularizing Jewish mysticism. In modern-day Israel, the followers are easily identified by their black suits and head coverings—either yarmulkes, kippahs, or shtreimels. The head coverings are based on the belief the "Divine Presence is always over their heads" and in covering their heads, they are "honoring God." They wear curls, known as *payot*, based on an interpretation of the biblical injunction against shaving the "corners" of one's head. Various styles of payot are worn by Heredi, Yemenite, and Hasidic Jews.

Hasmonean Dynasty – Named for the rebel leader and priest Mattathias, who began the overthrow of Seleucid rule leading to Jewish independence. The dynasty lasted for a hundred and three years before yielding to the Herodian Dynasty in 37 BC. It was one of the most glorious periods of Israel's history.

Hellenist – Culturally Greek

Herod Dynasty

- Herod the Great, founder of the dynasty who tried to kill the infant Jesus
- Herod Philip, son of Herod the Great and half-brother of Herod Antipas who ruled in southern Syria and Gaulanitis
- Herod Antipas, Tetrarch of Galilee and Perea who executed John the Baptist and before whom Jesus appeared when on trial
- Herod Archelaus of Judea, Samaria, and Idumea who was replaced by a series of Roman governors, including Pontius Pilate
- Herod Agrippa I who executed James the son of Zebedee and imprisoned Peter
- Herod Agrippa II who was appointed by Festus to hear Paul's defense

Immovable Ladder – Above the entrance to the Church of the Holy Sepulcher a ladder stands on a ledge belonging to the Armenian Church and rests on the sill of a window belonging to the Greek Orthodox part of the church. It is first mentioned as being there in 1757. Also known as the Stationary Ladder, it has remained because nothing can be changed in the church without consent of all groups who own parts of the church. No agreement has been reached in the hundreds of years of the Ladder's existence.

Israel – Named for one of the ancestors of the people known by that name. Jacob, the grandson of Abraham, had his name changed by God to Israel. His descendants eventually became known as the people of Israel, i.e. the descendants of Israel. Abraham and his descendants were presented as nomadic. The people of the region called such wandering Arameans *Apiry* (*Habiru*). In the language of Abraham's descendants, this word became *Ibri*, which was translated into English as Hebrew.

Jew – A person whose mother was a Jew or, according to Karaite Judaism, whose father was a Jew or one who had formally converted to Judaism through a recognized *beit din*.

Jewish Sects Today

- *Reform Judaism*: A modern movement which seeks to conform Jewish traditions to modern life allowing changes in the Halakhah.
- *Conservative Judaism*: A movement to adapt Judaism to modern life while following the laws. It is between Reform and Orthodox

Judaism.

- *Orthodox Judaism*: A strict traditional belief in keeping with the Torah and Halakha.
- *Reconstruction Judaism*: A broad Jewish group of great diversity. *Halakha*, the collective body of Jewish Law, is not considered binding, but valuable. They favor more modern trends.

Josephus – In Hebrew, Yosef ben Matityahu, a Jewish scholar, historian, and hagiographer, born in Jerusalem (37-100). Josephus was the commander of the revolt in Galilee. Turning their interest to Galilee, the Romans defeated his forces. He passed over to the Romans, and Vespasian made him the official chronicler of the Roman forces. He became a close friend of Vespasian and his son Titus; he went to Rome to live. There he wrote several books. The most important ones were *The Jewish Revolt Against Rome* and the *Antiquities of the Jews*.

Judahites – Term for the inhabitants of the Southern Kingdom of Judah after 922 BC.

Kotel – Means the wall and refers to the Western Wall of the Temple Mount. It is often simply called The Wall. For centuries, it has also been called the Wailing Wall where Jews came to wail for their sins and the destruction of the Temple. When the Jewish army entered Jerusalem in 1976, they immediately went to the Western Wall where they prayed and wept.

Kotel Tunnel – A tunnel that runs 1,591 feet along the base of the unearthed portion of the present two-hundred-foot exposed portion of the wall used for prayer, ending at the Via Dolorosa. The Western Stone, measuring forty-five feet long, almost ten feet high, and eleven feet wide, is exposed in the tunnel. Weighing over five hundred twenty metric tons, it is the largest object ever moved without mechanical means. Approximately one hundred fifty feet into the tunnel is Warren's Gate. It is the nearest point to the original Temple. Jews pray here to be near the Temple site.

Levant – *Levant* is an ancient name given the territories in the eastern Mediterranean region. Levant is from the French word *lever*, to rise as in sunrise, meaning in the east. Different countries are noted as being part of the Levant. Counties most often included are Syria, Lebanon, Jordan, and Israel and sometimes parts of Turkey, Iran, and Cyprus. It has been fought over so many times that it is considered the most blood-drenched land in the world, especially the Coastal Plain.

Maccabees – Jewish rebel warriors who seized control of Judea, which at the time was part of the Seleucid Empire. They resisted Greek polytheism, and in 164 BC they recaptured Jerusalem and purified the Temple. Hanukkah, the Jewish Festival of Lights, celebrates the Maccabean revolt (167-160 BC).

Mamelukes – Originally enslaved bodyguards of the Abbasid caliphs of the Islamic Empire. The name means king. Under the leadership of Ahm ibn Tulun, they revolted against their slave masters and became savage warriors, taking over Egypt in 870 BC. By 877 BC, they had conquered the Mediterranean coast including Israel and Syria.

Menorah – The original Jewish menorah begun by Moses in the portable sanctuary in the wilderness. It became a fixture in the Temple in Jerusalem. It had seven branches which were lit by Kohanim (priests) in the Temple during Bible time. Today a nine-candle menorah is used to celebrate Hanukkah, the defeating of the Syrians, and the reviving of the Temple in Jerusalem. The celebration lasts eight days to mark the eight days the oil miraculously burned in the Temple. It involves lighting one candle a day for eight days. A ninth candle depicts the servant candle used to light the others.

Mishnah – The code of Jewish law compiled in Sepphoris in 200. It is the compilation of authoritative doctrinal material consisting of the oral tradition of Jewish law.

Mitzvah – Codified Jewish law, commandments (Halakha).

Nabataeans – Arab people who inhabited northern Arabia and the Southern Levant with their capitol in Petra.

Ophel – An attractive high area just inside the Dung Gate on the southern side of the Temple Mount where there are remains of shops, stalls, ritual baths, cisterns, and residents dating from Bible time. Also, there is the impressive staircase leading to the Hulda Gates to the Temple Mount.

Petra – The sheer rock face of Mount Jabal Al-Bbah, one of history's most unique cities. Nearly two thousand years ago the Nabataeans settled in this basin of the mountains that run from the Dead Sea to the Gulf of Aqaba in southern Jordan. They developed the city as a vital junction on the silk, spice, and other trade routes linking China and India with Arabia, Syria, Egypt, Greece and Rome. Entrance to the city is through a mile-long narrow Siq overshadowed by high cliff walls. The first thing visible upon entering is the massive Al-Khazneh (Treasury) carved in the rose-red cliffs. Ornate dwellings and tombs are carved throughout the valley. Its decline was caused gradually by a series of events:

- First, the Roman arrival in 63 BC changed the culture.
- The Nabataeans were highly skilled at conserving water. A series of canals, locks, dams, and cisterns enabled them to have large deposits of water. A massive flood broke the system and flooded the valley, further depleting it.
- An extreme earthquake in 336 spoiled much of the area, causing the residents to move out onto a large plain where they survived for some time.
- Muslim conquests in the early seventh century resulted in a change of caravan routes cutting Petra off from the world. This led to the end of the culture.

Pharisees – A group of influential Jews active from second century BC through the first century BC. They were proponents of Sabbath rest, ritual purity, tithing, and dieting according to the Hebrew Scripture. The Apostle Paul is the only undisputed first century Pharisee from whom there are written records.

Phasael Tower – Located just inside the Jaffa Gate by the Citadel. It was one of three towers built by Herod on the north side of the Citadel and named for Herod's brother. From the top of these towers, it was possible to see and control the city and the surroundings of Jerusalem. Herod's magnificent palace extended to the south of these towers.

Phylactery – A small leather box containing Hebrew texts on vellum worn by Jewish men on their left arm and head, bound by leather thongs, at morning prayers and as a reminder to keep the Law. The texts were derived by rabbis based on Deuteronomy 6:8, 11:18, and Exodus 13: 9, 13.

Publicans – The title translates the Greek word *telones*, meaning tax collector. They were often ruthless and in general despised and hated. They later became tax farmers who made money by exacting excessive taxes.

Rabbi – A respected Jewish scholar or teacher. Jesus is the first person in recorded history to be called Rabbi.

Sabra – A nickname for a native-born Israeli Jew.

Saducees – A smaller group of elite and influential Jews living concurrently with the Pharisees.

Saladin – The first sultan of Egypt and Syria, a Sunni Muslim of Kurdish ethnicity. He led the Muslim military campaign against the Crusaders, proving himself to be a brilliant military strategist. His victory over the Crusaders in the battle at the Horns of Hattin resulted in the Christian Kingdom of Jerusalem falling.

Samaritans – Descendants of the ten Northern Tribes, the Kingdom of Israel, which separated from the two Southern Tribes of Judah and Benjamin after the death of Solomon (930 BC). Their region and capital city were both called Samaria.

Seleucides – Named for one of Alexandria's generals, Seleucus. They fought with the Tolomees for power in Israel.

Shabbat – From the root *Shin-Bet-Tav*, meaning to cease, to end, to rest. Also known as Sabbath, it is the seventh day of the week beginning at sunset Friday and ending at sunset Saturday.

Shema – The central statement of the Jewish faith: *Yisrael onai Elohaynu onai Ech*. Translated, it is "Hear, O Israel: the Lord our God, the Lord is one!" (Deuteronomy 6: 4). It means to listen.

Synagogue – Greek, Hebrew term meaning house of assembly, the Jewish place for prayer and study.

Talmud – The oral Torah was the foundation of Rabbinic Jewish Law. It has two components: the Mishnah, a written component of Rabbinic Judaism's Oral Law, and the Gemara, an elucidation of the Law.

Temple, Second – Built by decree of King Cyrus of Persia. He released the Jews from captivity, and they returned to build the Second Temple. It stood on the Holy Mount between 516 BC and 70.

Zealots – Founded by Judas the Galilean, a party which aggressively sought to defend Jewish Law and lifestyle against the Romans. A small segment was called Sicarii because of the practice of carrying a concealed dagger, a *Sicae*, used to kill anyone considered to be committing a sacrilegious act.

Zionism – The movement intent on reestablishing the modern Jewish state and further protecting it. It was established as a political organization in 1897 under Theodor Herzi and later led by Chaim Weizmann. It reached a zenith on May 14, 1948, when the Jewish People's Council assembled at the Tel Aviv Museum declared the establishment of the State of Israel. Zionism is Israel's ideology. Zionists believe Judaism is a nationality as well as a religion.

MAP Of ISRAEL

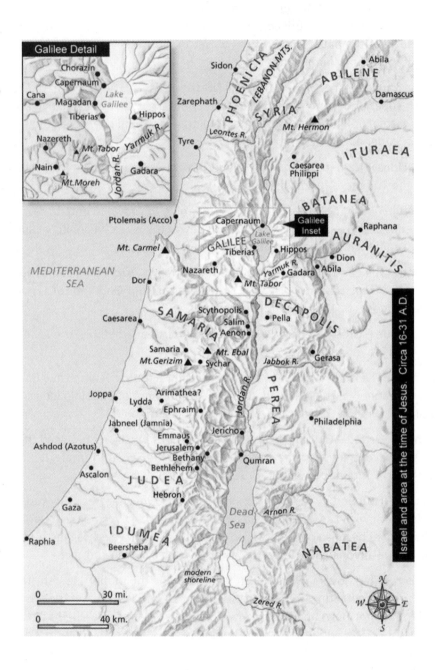